Flexibility in Academic Staffing:
Effective Policies and Practices

by Kenneth P. Mortimer, Marque Bagshaw, and Andrew T. Masland

ASHE-ERIC Higher Education Report No. 1, 1985

Prepared by

 ® *Clearinghouse on Higher Education*
The George Washington University

Published by

Association for the Study of Higher Education

Jonathan D. Fife,
Series Editor

Cite as:
Mortimer, Kenneth P.; Bagshaw, Marque; and Masland, Andrew T. *Flexibility in Academic Staffing: Effective Policies and Practices.* ASHE-ERIC Higher Education Report No. 1. Washington, D.C.: Association for the Study of Higher Education, 1985.

The ERIC Clearinghouse on Higher Education invites individuals to submit proposals for writing monographs for the Higher Education Report series. Proposals must include:
1. A detailed manuscript proposal of not more than five pages.
2. A 75-word summary to be used by several review committees for the initial screening and rating of each proposal.
3. A vita.
4. A writing sample.

Library of Congress Catalog Card Number: 85-72832
ISSN 0884-0040
ISBN 0-913317-20-9

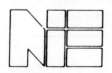

ERIC® **Clearinghouse on Higher Education**
The George Washington University
One Dupont Circle, Suite 630
Washington, D.C. 20036

ASHE Association for the Study of Higher Education
One Dupont Circle, Suite 630
Washington, D.C. 20036

This publication was partially prepared with funding from the National Institute of Education, U.S. Department of Education, under contract no. 400-82-0011. The opinions expressed in this report do not necessarily reflect the positions or policies of NIE or the Department.

EXECUTIVE SUMMARY

For the last decade, colleges and universities have been operating in intense conditions of scarce resources and environmental uncertainty. In response, institutions have experimented with more aggressive recruitment of students, redesigned programs to make students more job oriented, expanded development, tightened controls on expenditures, controlled enrollment in high-demand programs, and deferred maintenance on buildings and equipment.

One major result has been almost frantic attempts to experiment with different modes of academic staffing, most of which are attempts to preserve or create more flexible policies and practices. The literature and national conferences of academic administrators are filled with discussions on alternatives to tenure, the proper use of part-time faculty, incentives for early retirement, retraining faculty, and retrenchment.

More flexible strategies should not be used to justify the retrenchment of tenured or tenure-track faculty, however. The retrenchment of tenured faculty should be considered only as a last resort and only by institutions that have been stripped of their budgetary flexibility and lack other options for bringing programs into line with students' needs.

What Staffing Practices Are Being Used?
Although tenure systems are operative in 94 percent of all four-year colleges and universities and about 57 percent of all full-time faculty are tenured, tenure per se is not an insurmountable barrier to increased flexibility. Institutions have at least four major opportunities to reduce expenditures or to reallocate personnel:

1. The decision to create a position or to hire replacements for faculty leaving the institution (position control);
2. The decision about the type of appointment to be made (conversion to a no-tenure system, use of non-tenure tracks, and part-time appointments);
3. The decision to reduce the rate at which tenure-track faculty receive tenure (tenure quotas, extended probationary periods, suspension of the "up-or-out" rule, stricter standards for awarding tenure);

4. The decision to increase the number of tenured faculty leaving the institution (posttenure performance review, incentives for early retirement, retrenchment) or to convert underused tenured faculty to more productive use (faculty retraining programs).

The decision to create or fill a position is an essential ingredient in fiscal—as well as personnel—management. The key issue in managing positions through attrition is establishing a review of vacated positions that considers both institutionwide and departmental needs.

Fixed-term and/or rolling contracts provide an opportunity to achieve greater flexibility in staffing. Little evidence supports the view that such contracts stimulate faculty turnover, however, although they do limit the institution's fiscal commitment to the position to a relatively short period of time.

In the fall of 1981, 65 percent of four-year colleges and universities had full-time faculty on non-tenure-track appointments. These non-tenure-track appointments accounted for 12 percent of all full-time faculty. They allow institutions to hedge their long-term support for the position yet encourage faculty members to devote full time to teaching and research.

Approximately 25 percent of all faculty teaching in four-year colleges and universities are employed part time. The use of part-timers permits institutions to gain important savings, increases the opportunity for institutions to respond to changing student and curricular needs, and provides an important buffer against fluctuations in enrollment.

The tenure quota is one of the more common devices for limiting the number of tenured faculty; almost 30 percent of the institutions in the Project on Reallocation had a quota. The quota is simple to administer, promotes flexibility, tends to encourage selectivity and rigor, and may keep costs down. Some argue, however, that quotas are inequitable, encourage rapid turnover, discourage institutional commitment by young faculty members, and actually are inflexible and rigid.

The use of longer or extended probationary periods provides the opportunity to defer decisions about tenure. Adopting stricter standards for tenure may keep tenure ratios lower. These two practices are difficult to implement; they are seldom supported by faculty and may in effect have all the strengths and weaknesses of quotas.

The systematic review of tenured faculty occurs in slightly more than half of the four-year colleges and universities. About 3 percent of the 318 institutions in the sample actually use such reviews to terminate tenured faculty.

Institutions may use at least five types of incentives to encourage faculty to retire early: increased benefits, lump-sum payments, enhanced annuities, phased retirement, and continuation of fringe benefits. Less than 30 percent of the institutions have a formal early retirement program. Incentives for early retirement can be a useful tool in a limited number of cases, may have one-time, short-term effects on the composition of a faculty, and are complex to administer equitably.

Of the 16 percent of institutions that reported retrenching faculty, about half cited program closure or reduction and declining enrollments as the reasons. *Bona fide* financial exigency and program closure are legitimate grounds for retrenchment, but the use of program *reduction* as a reason to dismiss tenured faculty is highly controversial.

One of the least used devices for gaining curricular flexibility is retraining faculty through granting paid leaves. Even so, about 17 percent of the institutions are retraining faculty for new or revised assignments. Institutions have few incentives to retrain faculty when sufficient trained faculty already are available in the marketplace.

A faculty flow model can clarify alternatives; it must be easily adaptable to changing circumstances and have the support of top management. To be successful, it must be kept simple. Even successful flow models, however, cannot make decisions; they are best used as management and planning *tools* to evaluate personnel and fiscal strategies.

How Effective Are Reallocation Strategies?
The discussion about the effectiveness of the four reallocation strategies clusters around three topics: the content and impact of budget cuts, the strengths and weaknesses of various devices for reduction and reallocation, and consultation processes.

Budget cuts are felt in both academic and nonacademic areas, and they put great pressure on existing systems of allocating resources and setting priorities. Decremental budgeting systems are very difficult to implement over the years because of political forces on and off campus.

Effective use of the various strategies requires good leadership, a reasonably consistent definition of the problems and opportunities, and realistic expectations as to what is possible. It usually is not reasonable, for example, to expect to save actual dollars by reorganizing or closing programs unless personnel are terminated. The most one might expect is to avoid future cost increases.

The process of reallocation is complex and should involve broad consultation. Consultation with faculty committees about reduction and reallocation tends to be most effective when faculty are asked about methods and criteria to be used rather than about specific programs or people.

How Can Institutions Become More Flexible?
Institutional flexibility should not be equated with institutional autonomy. No *single* policy or practice discussed here has the potential to restore flexibility in an institution. In the aggregate, however, the more effective management of *all* these practices and policies can lead to greater flexibility and, if matched with a three- to five-year perspective, can result in the institution's improved performance. Administrators would be wise to implement the following suggestions:

- Develop an appropriate and comprehensive institutional strategy.
- Know the institution.
- Know what the institution values.
- Temper expectations with realism.
- Link personnel and fiscal affairs.
- Match solutions to problems.
- Manage entry to the tenure track.
- Manage positions and develop people.
- Preserve managerial prerogatives by exercising them.

ADVISORY BOARD

CONSULTING EDITORS

Harold Orlans
Office of Programs and Policy
United States Civil Rights Commission

Lois S. Peters
Center for Science and Technology Policy
New York University

John M. Peterson
Director, Technology Planning
The B. F. Goodrich Company

Marianne Phelps
Assistant Provost for Affirmative Action
The George Washington University

Richard H. Quay
Social Science Librarian
Miami University

John E. Stecklein
Professor of Educational Psychology
University of Minnesota

Donald Williams
Professor of Higher Education
University of Washington

CONTENTS

FOREWORD

Fiscal responsibility is becoming the chief focus of government officials, business leaders, and now, college administrators. With a typical school expending 70%–80% of its operating budget on faculty and staff salaries, benefits, and pensions, budgetary control efforts naturally begin here. The ability to alter the faculty's composition on an annual basis is vital to ensuring the survivability of some schools, due to the wide fluctuations of normal revenue sources, such as uncertain federal and state support, problematic private giving, inflation, demographic shifts, and changing student course preferences. Flexibility in academic staffing is one method by which administrators can retain academic excellence without incurring excessive or long-term expenses. Flexibility in academic staffing means the old stepladder system from assistant professor through associate professor to full professor will not exist for every faculty position. Although tenure is justified and meritorious, maintaining the pace of tenure-track assignments is impossible when fully 57% of the professors at four-year colleges and universities are tenured. Administrators can help control their shrinking budgets by hiring more part-time faculty members, using either fixed-term or rolling contracts, employing non-tenured-track personnel, or absorbing some tenured positions as faculty members retire. Agreement will have to be reached between faculty and administrators before any option can work harmoniously.

The authors are especially qualified to address the issue of staffing practices. Under a grant from the Lilly Endowment administered through the Teachers Insurance and Annuity Association/College Retirement Equities Fund, Kenneth Mortimer, vice president and vice provost of The Pennsylvania State University, directed the Project on Reallocation in Higher Education, assisted by Marque Bagshaw and Annette Caruso. The project was the basis for much of the information contained in this report. Dr. Mortimer, Dr. Bagshaw, the executive assistant to the president at Clark University, and Andrew Masland, senior marketing specialist at Digital Equipment Corporation—all formerly of the Center for the Study of Higher Education at the Pennsylvania State University—focus on three main areas. First, they consider the environmental conditions that have brought about this state of affairs. Second, they compare 13 specific academic staffing practices, and finally, recommend ways that administrators and faculty can best implement these procedures. The benefits and disadvantages of each option are discussed in turn, thereby producing a comprehensive examination of the issues.

It is with great pleasure that we introduce our fourteenth series with this issue. To more accurately reflect the aim of this series, we have changed the title to the ASHE-ERIC Higher Education Reports. We remain committed to producing for the higher education community timely reports that synthesize and analyze the major literature and institutional practices.

Jonathan D. Fife
Series Editor
Professor and Director
ERIC Clearinghouse on Higher Education
The George Washington University

ACKNOWLEDGMENTS

The conduct of a project requires much collaboration and joint effort. Dr. Peggy Heim of TIAA/CREF has been a constant source of ideas and counsel throughout the life of the Project on Reallocation. She reacted to the original proposal, served on the advisory committee, and commented on a draft of the manuscript. We have found her to be a good colleague and friend.

The Project on Reallocation was funded by Lilly Endowment, Inc., and Ralph Lundgren's support is appreciated. The project advisory committee reacted to early design questions and considered some of the early findings. We wish to thank its members: David Brown, Marina Bühler-Miko, Elaine El-Khawas, Jerry Gaff, Peggy Heim, and Wendel Smith.

We value the opportunity to work closely with such highly able colleagues as Annette Caruso, Leslie Haskins, and Thomas Ritchey. In 1982, they coordinated and conducted over 300 telephone interviews. In addition, Thomas Ritchey managed the creation of the data file, and Ann Caruso and Robert Rutchik helped with some of the data analysis.

In 1983, the senior author was supported by TIAA and the Exxon Education Foundation to examine reduction and reallocation problems in England. While those results are not reported here, the trip helped formulate the discussion strategies, and this support is gratefully acknowledged.

The manuscript was typed and retyped by Karen Bruno at Penn State. My secretary, Joan Summers, supervised the entire process with her usual care and efficiency.

Peggy Heim and Jerry Gaff reviewed the final manuscript and made several helpful suggestions. Naturally we assume full responsibility for advice taken and for advice ignored!

Finally, we appreciate Jonathan Fife's patience with the many delays.

INTRODUCTION

Given the prevailing conditions of scarce resources and environmental uncertainty, institutions of higher education need to become more flexible in academic staffing and to develop personnel strategies that will serve them well in allocating resources. The pursuit of flexibility, however, should not be used to justify the wholesale retrenchment of tenured and tenure-track faculty members. Most institutions are firmly committed to the principles and practices of academic tenure, and the retrenchment of tenured faculty should be carried out only as a last resort and only by institutions that have been stripped of budgetary flexibility and lack other, more humane options for bringing expenditures and programs into line with revenues and students' needs. The development of reasonable flexibility is consistent with the development of reasonable numbers of highly qualified tenure-track faculty.

Four general factors may limit an institution's flexibility in attempting to manage scarce resources and to adapt to environmental uncertainty: (1) excessive external budgetary controls, (2) limited time to respond to change, (3) limited capacity to reallocate resources, and (4) internal opposition.

Institutions that depend on state appropriations for operating revenues often are constrained by state-imposed budgetary policies and practices. The fiscal and administrative controls include:

1. *The authority of institutions to carry funds forward from one year to the next, to expend excess income, and to invest funds;*
2. *The procedures imposed on procurement, contracting, disposal of property, and personnel policy;*
3. *The authority to reallocate funds among categories of appropriations during the budget year;*
4. *The special review processes established for sensitive areas, such as purchasing data-processing equipment and traveling;*
5. *The monitoring and regulation of hiring through [state-level] "position control"* (Mingle 1983, p. 5).

Other external constraints include the mandatory return to the state of salaries saved when positions are vacated and elaborate mechanisms for securing external approval to

---

close academic programs. Although intended to achieve coordination of public services and accountability in the expenditure of public funds, these policies and practices may limit an institution's staffing flexibility.

The need to move rapidly in response to environmental change may also impose limits on an institution's flexibility. A public institution that has developed a detailed, multiyear plan for reducing expenditures, for example, may find these plans wiped out by a sudden and unexpected mid-year recision of its state appropriation.

Many institutions have limited capacity to reallocate resources because of the small scale of their operations or because of the magnitude of their long-term commitment of resources in the form of tenure obligations. One of the assumptions implicit in most reallocation strategies is that funds and positions can be taken from one area of an institution and allocated to another area without jeopardizing the institution's essential viability. Although a large institution can create a substantial pool of resources for reallocation by marginal assessments of its typically large number of subunits or by significant selective reduction of some units, a small institution frequently lacks a broad enough budget base to accumulate resources for large-scale reallocation. Small liberal arts institutions in particular may be unable to discriminate easily between the essential and the expendable in their academic programs (because no part of the curriculum is expendable) and may be unable to garner substantial amounts to reallocate from one corner of the institution to another.

Tenure decisions represent long-term salary commitments and are reinforced by strong professional, traditional, and ethical norms that are difficult to quantify. In the aggregate, tenure commitments may limit an institution's capacity to reallocate funds internally. A decision to tenure a 35-year-old faculty member, for example, probably will cost more than $1 million by the time the professor retires (Chait 1984, p. 25). Under conditions of declining resources and environmental uncertainty, the most meaningful measure of whether tenure levels at an institution are too high is the extent to which the commitment of the institution's resources to existing tenured positions prevents the institution from maintaining or developing the capacity to reallocate resources.

Internal opposition to decisions to reallocate resources can significantly reduce staffing flexibility. Institutions with organized faculties may be unable to avoid bargaining away some flexibility in contract negotiations and may be constrained by a formal contractual agreement to use some staffing options in preference to others. Academic deans and department heads who stand to lose funds or positions by certain staffing options will seldom think implementing such options to be fair or wise. Governmental agencies, special-interest groups, accrediting organizations, and alumni can become effective political allies of those within the institution who are opposed to changes in staffing policies or to the reallocation of resources. Institutional leaders may find the same arguments they use in seeking greater freedom from external control used against them by their own academic units.

Many of the observations in this work derive directly from the analysis of data gathered by the Project on Reallocation in Higher Education, a national study of the methods and extent of institutional efforts to reallocate resources (see Mortimer, Bagshaw, and Caruso 1985). Since 1982, the Project on Reallocation has gathered information on the prevailing faculty staffing practices in four-year colleges and universities, identified patterns of reallocation and reduction, and analyzed the implications of these practices and patterns. The project reviewed published and fugitive literature on academic staffing and reallocation, conducted site visits at nine institutions, and interviewed the chief academic officers (or their designates) at 318 respondent institutions in a telephone survey of 369 randomly selected four-year colleges and universities (an 86 percent response rate). Interview data were matched with other institutional information, such as enrollment history, Carnegie classification, and type of control. The 318 institutions that provided data for the survey represented slightly more than 23 percent of the population of U.S. four-year colleges and universities, excluding professional schools and other specialized institutions.

Thus, this work includes observations from national and from campus-based perspectives, a rather comprehensive literature review, and other studies of institutional adaptations (see, for example, Bagshaw 1984; Johnson and Mortimer 1977; Mortimer 1981; Mortimer, Bagshaw, and Caruso 1985; Mortimer and Ladd 1981; Mortimer and Taylor 1984;

Mortimer and Tierney 1979). It is organized in three main sections. The first section briefly reviews the environmental conditions that have contributed to institutions' budgetary problems and outlines the broad framework within which institutions have sought to develop strategies for coping with these conditions. The second section examines 13 specific academic staffing practices in some detail, typically describing the practice, the extent to which it is currently used among four-year colleges and institutions, and the important considerations in an institution's decision to use the practice. The second section also includes a discussion of faculty flow models as a management and planning tool in evaluating personnel and fiscal strategies and a general discussion of reallocation and reduction strategies. The final section offers a number of recommendations for institutions seeking to maintain or increase their flexibility in staffing.

THE INSTITUTIONAL CONTEXT

In the mid-1980s, the dominant feature of the institutional context is uncertainty in the face of scarce resources. This situation derives from a combination of demographic and economic conditions and projections that have been discussed frequently in the literature (see, for example, Carnegie Council 1980; Mortimer and Tierney 1979; Stadtman 1980) and may be encountered differently in different institutional settings:

1. *Smaller numbers of potential college students in the traditional college-age population.* Nationally, the number of individuals in the U.S. population aged 18 to 24 reached a high of about 30.4 million in 1981 and is projected by the U.S. Bureau of the Census to decline by 5.6 percent to 28.7 million in 1985, and by 22.0 percent to 23.7 million in 1995, before climbing slightly and leveling off at about 25 million near the year 2000 (American Council on Education 1984, p. 4). The number of 18-year-olds in the population peaked in 1979 at 4.3 million and is projected to decline by 14.0 percent to 3.7 million in 1985, and by 23.3 percent to 3.3 million in 1995, before rising to the 1984 level of 3.8 million in the year 2000 and dropping only slightly on an annual basis thereafter (American Council on Education 1984, p. 5).

Although total enrollment at all institutions of higher education has grown from 11 million in the fall of 1976 to 12.46 million in 1983 (a 13.6 percent increase), the rate of annual growth has slowed. The record fall 1983 enrollment represents only a modest 0.3 percent gain over the fall 1982 figures, and preliminary analysis of fall 1984 enrollments suggests that 1984 will be close to the 1983 total of 12.46 million (Evangelauf 1984, p. 1). While future college rates of attendance remain uncertain, the direct impact of potentially fewer college students is that revenues from tuition and fees may decline proportionally as a result "solely [of] a decline in the number of persons paying that tuition" (Mortimer and Tierney 1979, p. 9).

2. *Uncertain federal support.* The federal share of the burden of financing educational and general institutional purposes decreased from 23 to 16 percent, nationally, in the 1970s (Carnegie Council 1980, pp. 11–12). By 1980–81, the percentage derived from the federal government for these purposes had declined to 14.9 percent (American Council on Education 1984, p. 45).

. . . the dominant feature of the institutional context is uncertainty in the face of scarce resources.

Federal support for higher education in the form of funds to perform research averaged about 1.8 percent of the U.S. gross national product (GNP) in the 1960s and about 1.3 percent of the GNP in the 1970s, rising at the end of the decade (Carnegie Council 1980, p. 125). Changes in federal guidelines for research have reduced the amount of institutional expenditures recoverable by institutions as indirect costs of federal grants and contracts (Roark 1978). Federal agencies have in recent years increasingly shifted to smaller grants and short-term research commitments, "with seriously destabilizing effects" on university research (National Commission 1983, p. 52).

The federal government is debating the level of support to be given students. Federal student aid policy in recent years has placed more of the burden of financing a college education onto the student, with an as-yet-undetermined effect on rates of attendance and on institutional budgets.

3. *Uncertainty in state appropriations.* Although it varies widely by state and region, the rate of growth in state appropriations to colleges and universities has not been constant across states or over time, both because of economic conditions that have reduced tax revenues and because of a general devaluation of higher education as a state funding priority during the 1970s (Mortimer and Tierney 1979, p. 12). On the average, state appropriations to colleges and universities in 1983 showed the smallest one-year increase, 6.2 percent, in more than 20 years (Magarrell 1983, p. 1). While some states have had more robust budgets and have increased their appropriations recently, the long-range outlook is uncertain. A preliminary report by the National Governors Association and the National Association of State Budget Officers indicates that the growth of state tax revenues is expected to slow in the next two years (Magarrell 1984). State-assisted institutions in several states have experienced the destabilizing effects of mid-year recisions of their state funds when state tax revenues fell as the result of unanticipated economic downturns.

4. *Problematic private giving.* In total dollar amount, voluntary support of institutions of higher education has increased every year since 1975, but the purchasing power of this support in constant dollars increased by only about 9 percent between 1975–76 and 1981–82 (American Council on Education 1984, p. 43). Historically, private giving has

increased with increased economic productivity and decreased during economic recession (Mortimer and Tierney 1979, p. 13), and the results of institutional efforts at private fund raising are conditioned by uncertainty in the economy. Furthermore, the percentage of institutional income derived from private giving has remained modest and fairly stable during the past decade: 4.9 percent of current fund income in 1974–75, 4.8 percent in 1978–79, and 4.8 percent in 1980–81 (American Council on Education 1984, p. 45). Despite "heroic" institutional efforts and expenditures to significantly expand or retool development programs, growth in revenues from gifts is unlikely to offset declining revenues in other areas.

5. *Inflation.* Double-digit inflation in the 1970s severely eroded the purchasing power of institutions. The higher education price index, which uses 1967 prices as an index to measure the effects of changing prices on a fixed group of goods and services purchased by colleges and universities, rose from 121.0 at the end of fiscal 1970 to 238.3 by the end of fiscal 1980 (American Council on Education 1984, p. 31). Faculty salaries did not keep pace with inflation in the 1970s and fell behind salary levels for comparable positions in other professions and in business (Heim 1980). While the costs of operating and maintaining classrooms, dormitories, and other physical plant, and the costs of library and laboratory materials, supplies, and research equipment continue to rise in the 1980s at a lower rate, many institutions have yet to fully recover from past fiscal stringencies brought on by the last economic recession. These institutions badly need to repair plant, replace equipment, and adjust faculty compensation to *restore* some measure of academic quality and institutional vitality.

6. *Increased accountability costs.* Demands for accountability by legislatures and government agencies and for compliance with other mandated programs, such as affirmative action and equal employment opportunity, and greater willingness to resort to legal action on the part of students, faculty, and external agencies have added costs in the form of new record-keeping functions and additional support personnel.

7. *Increased faculty costs.* The enormous growth in the size of the professoriate in the 1960s, the proportionate growth in the tenured ranks, the near-zero growth in job

openings for faculty in the late 1970s and early 1980s, and the extension of compulsory retirement to age 70 through the Age Discrimination in Employment Act have helped to create a situation in which the professoriate has grown older, relatively immobile, difficult to reduce in size, and more expensive to employ. Fringe benefits (including institutional contributions to social security) have become an increasingly larger percentage of institutional costs. According to a report by TIAA/CREF, the average expenditure of four-year colleges and universities for employee retirement and insurance benefits in 1984 was 18.6 percent of payroll costs, compared with 18 percent in 1981. Social security taxes and other mandatory employer payments averaged 6.4 percent of payroll in 1984, compared with 6 percent in 1981 (Jacobson 1985, p. 27).

8. *Shifts in students' course preferences.* The shift in students' preferences that began in the 1970s for more narrowly job-oriented courses of study has created staffing and funding imbalances between high- and low-demand areas of study (Stadtman 1980). This situation has given many institutions the choice of making additional expenditures for faculty, instructional and laboratory facilities, and sophisticated equipment in some high-demand areas (such as computer science) or capping enrollments in those areas, thereby closing off one valuable source of additional revenue. Regardless of the choice, these institutions must still deal with continuing to employ and pay faculty in low-demand areas of study.

These conditions, as stated earlier, are unlikely to affect every institution to the same degree or in the same way. For example, with regard to enrollment patterns, the Project on Reallocation survey found that *growth* in enrollment was the dominant experience of four-year colleges and universities over the period 1972 to 1981 (Mortimer, Bagshaw, and Caruso 1985, p. 10). At about 69 percent of respondent institutions in that study, enrollment increased 5 percent or more (the enrollment "gainers") over the period, and at only 20 percent of respondent institutions, enrollment decreased 5 percent or more (the enrollment "decliners"). The remaining 11 percent of respondent institutions experienced enrollment decreases or increases of less than 5 percent (the "stable enrollment" institutions). Various institutional types experience significantly different enrollment (see table 1). A larger percentage of doctorate-granting institutions gained enrollment (81 percent), and a larger percentage of liberal arts colleges (28 percent) experienced declining enrollment.

TABLE 1
CHANGE IN FTE ENROLLMENT, FALL 1972 TO FALL 1981, BY CARNEGIE CLASSIFICATION[a]

Carnegie Classification[b]	Growth		Stable		Decline	
	N	%	N	%	N	%
1.0 Doctorate-granting	34	81	3	7	5	12
2.0 Comprehensives	101	74	15	11	21	15
3.0 Liberal arts colleges	80	60	16	12	37	28
Totals[c]	**215**	**69**	**34**	**11**	**63**	**20**

[a]Change is defined as at least 5 percent growth or decline in FTE enrollment.
[b]For a discussion of specific Carnegie classifications, see Carnegie Council 1976.
[c]Six of the 318 institutions in the sample did not exist in 1972. This range of Carnegie classification categories includes all U.S. four-year colleges and universities, excluding professional schools and other specialized institutions.

Source: The Project on Reallocation (Mortimer, Bagshaw, and Caruso 1985).

INSTITUTIONAL COPING STRATEGIES

Institutions seeking to manage scarce resources have a limited number of strategies they can develop: generate additional revenues, reduce expenditures, reallocate internal resources to produce institutional services more efficiently, or do all three.

To generate revenues, some institutions have experimented with more aggressive recruitment of both traditional college-age and older clienteles, and some have lowered or adopted more flexible admissions policies to increase enrollments. A number of institutions have begun to hire directors of "enrollment management"—a title that reflects a new emphasis on carrying out market research on prospective applicants and devising new admissions strategies. Some institutions have added more job-oriented programs to the curriculum and redesigned existing programs to appeal more directly to students. Many institutions have increased tuition while, in some cases, trying to project the number of students who may choose not to enroll at given levels of tuition increase. Almost every institution has attempted to revitalize or expand its development or private giving program in recent years.

On the other side of the ledger, options to reduce expenditures fall into two categories: those directed at curbing the rate of growth in expenditures and those directed at reducing the absolute size of annual budget expenditures. One way of curbing expenditures to deal with enrollment surges in areas like business, engineering, and computer science is to cap enrollments: Almost one-third of respondent institutions in the Project on Reallocation survey had initiated institutionwide or program-specific enrollment caps. The use of enrollment caps appears to be concentrated in certain types of institutions: Almost two-thirds of the respondent doctorate-granting institutions had capped enrollment, whereas over 80 percent of liberal arts colleges had not. Doctorate-granting universities were significantly more likely to have used this management device to control or limit imbalances resulting from student demand. Caps on specific programs accounted for 70 percent of reported enrollment caps.

Some institutions have attempted to reduce the growth of nonacademic expenditures by more efficient operations, purchasing, and scheduling and by deferring expenditures like normal maintenance of physical plant and purchase of new and replacement equipment. Maintenance cannot be deferred indefinitely, however, and deferred purchase of equipment in instructional and research areas may jeopardize research and instructional quality.

These savings, while significant, do not alter the fact that *faculty and supporting staff salaries, wages, and fringe benefits may constitute 70 to 80 percent of an institution's operating budget expenditures* (Mortimer and Tierney 1979, p. 35). Thus, important opportunities for reducing the growth of expenditures lie in the area of salaries—cutting salaries, freezing salaries, reducing (or ''deferring'') salary increments, collapsing vacant positions, reducing the number of personnel, and adopting alternatives to tenure-track staffing.

Because the greater part of an institution's budget is devoted to academic salaries, efforts to significantly reduce the absolute size of budget expenditures focus on academic areas. Basically, an institution has two options: to change student/faculty ratios or to change the composition of the faculty so as to lower the total dollar amount of faculty costs. Increasing the number of students while holding the number of faculty constant is essentially a strategy to generate revenue; holding the number of students constant while decreasing the number of faculty is a strategy to reduce expenditures. Both may adversely affect faculty and student morale and the quality of advising and instruction. Nonetheless, reducing the number of faculty and the number of faculty positions by collapsing vacant positions, retrenchment, or seeking early retirements has become a necessity for some institutions.

Tenure commitments add to the difficulty of reducing budget expenditures by decreasing the number of faculty. Based on the results of the Project on Reallocation survey, 94 percent of American four-year colleges and universities have a tenure system, and 57 percent of all full-time faculty at four-year institutions are tenured. Efforts to change the composition of an institution's faculty to reduce the long-term costs of tenure commitments have included use of part-time and non-tenure-track appointments, implementation of tenure quotas, and tougher enforcement of criteria for tenure and promotion (or new, tougher criteria).

Internal reallocation of funds is an area where institutions have the most flexibility when the growth of revenues declines, largely because funds are a liquid resource (Carnegie Council 1975, p. 87; Shapiro 1978, p. 21). Faculty members, however, are a relatively illiquid resource; they cannot be divested or reallocated easily. As an extreme example, a tenured professor of classics with 15 years of service cannot be converted efficiently into an entry-level part-time instructor in computer science. Nevertheless, some institutions have converted underused tenured faculty members in areas of low student demand to more productive resources through faculty exchange programs and programs to retrain faculty for new assignments.

Thus a major problem for institutions seeking to reduce expenditures and to use revenues more efficiently is the problem of how to limit the growth or reduce the number of tenure commitments, make more flexible staffing arrangements, and reallocate faculty and thereby avoid paying an increasingly higher price for production resources that because of changes in student demand or because of tenure commitments might not be efficiently employed. The following section examines specific faculty staffing practices and general institutional strategies that address these issues.

Flexibility in Tenure and Staffing

Tenure remains the central feature of academic staffing policy on most U.S. campuses. Approximately 85 percent of all American colleges and universities, including two-year institutions, have tenure systems. About 59 percent of all full-time faculty have tenure (Chait and Ford 1982, p. ix). Ninety-four percent of four-year colleges and universities have tenure systems, and about 57 percent of all full-time faculty at four-year colleges and universities have tenure (Mortimer, Bagshaw, and Caruso 1985). Clearly, traditional tenure remains firmly in place (Di Biase 1979).

Some of the factors that perpetuate traditional tenure include (1) the pervasiveness of tenure systems among institutions of higher education, which discourages deviation from accepted practice; (2) the resilience of the principles of tenure of freedom and economic security against attack from external agents; (3) the legality of seniority; and (4) support for tenure systems by faculty unions (Chait 1979; Chait and Ford 1982).

With the onset of "no growth" and decline in the early 1970s, however, some institutions began to view their tenure ratios—the proportion of institutional faculty that is tenured—as impediments to responding to changed circumstances. A high tenure ratio, for example, is one indicator of potential danger in faculty personnel systems (Furniss 1974). If an institution has a high tenure ratio, it is argued, it will have more difficulty in opening or closing academic programs, freeing resources to respond to shifts in student demand, or improving the quality of existing programs and providing for institutional renewal by hiring new faculty.

One of the biggest problems associated with the use of tenure ratio as an indicator of staffing inflexibility is the lack of agreement on a standard measure. Most published works on the subject of tenure ratios do not state how the tenure ratio is defined, which leads to fuzzy thinking on the topic. Should the tenure ratio, for example, include only full-time faculty? Are all levels of instructional staff, including graduate assistants and visiting or temporary faculty, part of the calculation? Should the institution include administrators who no longer teach but continue to hold tenured appointments? Are only those individuals who hold tenure or who are eligible for tenure included in the

A high tenure ratio . . . is one indicator of potential danger in faculty personnel systems.

calculation, or should faculty members who are not eligible for tenure be included? The answers to these and similar questions can make large differences in calculations of the tenure ratio.

Which method of calculating tenure ratios is best depends on how and why the ratio is used. Many reports of tenure ratios appear to use a ratio of full-time tenured faculty divided by full-time tenured and tenure-track faculty. This ratio excludes part-time and tenure-ineligible instructional staff and in some cases gives the appearance of a decrease over time in institutional flexibility. As an alternative, an appropriate way to measure tenure ratio, if an institution is interested in measuring the extent to which the institutional budget is committed to tenured faculty, is the number of tenured faculty divided by total full-time equivalent (FTE) faculty, including graduate students who teach. In this case, the emphasis of the measure is on flexibility in total instructional staff.

Differences in calculating tenure ratio can affect the measure (and perception) of staffing flexibility. As shown in table 2, the Project on Reallocation found that, on the average, about 57 percent of all *full-time* faculty at four-year colleges and universities were tenured in fall 1981. Measuring the tenure ratio as the percentage of full-time faculty that is tenured, however, ignores the additional staffing flexibility many institutions have gained by using part-time faculty. When part-timers are taken into account and the tenure ratio is calculated as the percentage of FTE faculty that is tenured (with one part-time faculty member counted as one-third FTE), the mean FTE tenure ratio for four-year colleges and universities with tenure systems is about 50 percent; that is, although on the average 57 percent of full-time faculty are tenured, only about 50 percent of FTE faculty represent tenure commitments at tenure-awarding institutions.

An alternative method of measuring the extent of inflexibility related to tenure commitments is to examine the financial resources that tenured faculty consume rather than the number of tenured faculty on the campus. Institutions need flexibility in the overall budget or in the distribution of funds among programs, departments, schools, or colleges. Limiting the number of tenured faculty is, at best, an imprecise tool for increasing flexibility. The use of a

TABLE 2
ESTIMATE OF TENURED FACULTY AT FOUR-YEAR COLLEGES AND UNIVERSITIES

Faculty Data (Headcount), Fall 1981

		Full-time		Part-time		Total
		N	%	N	%	
Tenured	N	49,012	98.8	588	1.2	49,600
	%	57.4		2.0		43.5
Tenure-track	N	25,509	98.5	389	1.5	25,898
	%	29.9		1.3		22.7
Other[a]	N	10,843	28.1	27,750	71.9	38,593
	%	12.7		96.6		33.8
Totals		**85,364**	74.8	**28,727**	25.2	**114,091**
		100.0		100.0		100.0

National Estimate—Four-year Colleges and Universities (× 4.3)[b]

	Full-time	Part-time	Total
Tenured	210,752	2,528	213,280
Tenure-track	109,689	1,673	111,362
Other[a]	46,625	119,325	165,950
Totals	**367,066**	**123,526**	**490,592**

[a]"Other" includes both faculty on appointments at institutions that do not award tenure and faculty on non-tenure-track appointments at tenure-awarding institutions.
[b]Sample institutions represent slightly more than 23 percent of the populations of four-year colleges and universities; thus, the national estimates result from multiplying sample frequencies by a factor of 4.3.

Source: Mortimer, Bagshaw, and Caruso 1985.

financial tenure ratio that shows the proportion of funds used to support tenured faculty members may indicate that an institution is more or less flexible than the traditional tenure ratio demonstrates. It might also be useful for the institution to take "hard" and "soft" monies into account when calculating the financial ratios.

One factor that relates directly to the magnitude of tenure ratios is the rate at which tenure-eligible faculty are awarded tenure. Some evidence suggests that the rate of awarding tenure has contributed to higher tenure ratios at some institutions. A survey carried out for the Commission on Academic Tenure in Higher Education (1973) (the Keast Commission) found that 42 percent of respondent institutions (two-year and four-year) with tenure systems had granted tenure to all faculty members considered for tenure in the spring of 1971 and that two-thirds of the institutions had awarded tenure to 70 percent or more of faculty considered for tenure. In 1974, 65 percent of all institutions granted tenure to more than 60 percent of eligible faculty (El-Khawas and Furniss 1974). Of all full-time faculty considered for tenure at four-year colleges and universities in 1978–79, 58 percent received tenure, 22 percent remained eligible for reconsideration, and only 20 percent were denied tenure (Atelsek and Gomberg 1980).

One must temper this evidence of high rates of tenure award with the recognition that many of the least suitable candidates for tenure have been counseled out at earlier stages of the tenure probationary period. Well-managed tenure systems evaluate the performance of probationary faculty early and often, resulting in some voluntary resignations and nonreappointments before the tenure decision is reached. Thus, high rates of denying tenure at an institution may indicate not that high standards for tenure are being rigorously upheld but that the system for evaluating and advising probationary faculty about their progress and performance is not working well.

In 1978, tenure ratios at public and private four-year colleges and universities that award tenure (with tenure ratio calculated as full-time tenured faculty divided by total full-time faculty) were 69 percent and 63 percent, respectively (Atelsek and Gomberg 1980). When tenure ratios were calculated in the same way using Project on Reallocation faculty data for fall 1981, the tenure ratio at public four-year colleges and universities that award tenure was 61 percent, and the tenure ratio at private four-year institutions was 54 percent. Comparing these figures suggests that institutions may be less heavily tenured than earlier and that institutions may be modifying their staffing practices.

A complete set of faculty personnel policies covers all aspects of faculty employment—from the creation of a position and the appointment of a faculty member to fill it, through the stages of evaluation and reward of faculty performance in the position, to the termination of the position or the retirement of the faculty member. This discussion of specific staffing practices follows this developmental pattern of the employment relationship. In the course of that relationship, four major opportunities occur to reduce expenditures or reallocate resources and to increase institutional flexibility.

1. The decision to create a position or to hire replacements for faculty leaving the institution (position control);
2. The decision about the type of appointment to be made (conversion to a no-tenure system, use of nontenure tracks, and part-time appointments);
3. The decision to reduce the rate of tenure-track faculty receiving tenure (tenure quotas, extended probationary periods, suspension of the "up-or-out" rule, stricter standards for awarding tenure;
4. The decision to increase the number of tenured faculty leaving the institution (posttenure performance review, incentives for early retirement, retrenchment) or to convert underused tenured faculty to more productive use (faculty retraining programs).

These opportunities exist at all institutions. While some of the staffing practices employed to realize them are not "normative" in terms of principles of academic tenure widely supported in the profession, all have been employed by at least some institutions, and all have the potential to increase flexibility.

Control of Academic Positions by Attrition
One of the primary ways institutions have attempted to reduce the level of tenure commitments is through tighter control of tenure-track positions. A number of studies have reported that not filling a position when the incumbent resigns or is dismissed remains the most commonly employed method of controlling positions and reducing the number of faculty (Mortimer, Caruso, and Ritchey 1982, p. 13). When the incumbent faculty member leaves, the position is simply erased. In a 1974 study of staff reduction policies at 163 institutions in 14 different states, not filling

vacancies was the most common method of reducing staff (Sprenger and Schultz 1974). The University of California–Riverside "absorbed" 42 positions and the University of Wisconsin–Eau Claire 30 through attrition (Dougherty 1979, 1980a, 1980b).

The crucial debate over controlling faculty positions through attrition centers on deciding who has the ultimate authority to collapse or to fill or create a position. "While several different approaches can be used, practically all of them are variations of two basic types of fiscal management systems, either (1) giving deans and other equivalent administrative officers both the total responsibility for control of how to spend the funds assigned to them, or (2) centrally controlling major expenditure of funds" (Fortunato and Waddell 1981, p. 12). In the Project on Reallocation survey, respondents were asked whose approval must be gained before a vacant faculty position can be refilled. Almost 85 percent replied that the *campus* administration's approval is necessary.

The fundamental point is that the decision to fill or create a position is an essential ingredient in a system of *fiscal* management. In some institutions in the Project on Reallocation survey, the decision to *create* a tenure-track position was, in nine out of 10 cases, a de facto commitment to tenure for the person hired. For example, until 1981–82, the collective bargaining agreement and actual practices in the 14 campuses of the Pennsylvania state college system placed the burden of proof on the institution, after the first semester, if tenure were to be denied. Instead of the tenure candidate's being required to demonstrate performance that would justify the awarding of tenure, the institution had to demonstrate that the candidate's performance was inadequate and to specify what its standards of adequate performance were. One can easily imagine cases where this requirement is difficult to perform.

The focus of the tenure decision under such circumstances tends to shift away from the qualitative and subjective judgment of professional peers to a more "objective" and quantitative measurement of tenure worthiness in which tenure candidates are "scored" on a battery of performance indicators. This method puts the institution in the position of having to defend the validity of its performance indicators, its definition of what constitutes an adequate score for awarding tenure, and the score that is assigned to the tenure candidate. Any or all might be assailed as arbitrary or capricious. Thus, when institutions must demonstrate inadequate performance as a basis for denying tenure and when quantifiable measures take the place of professional judgment in tenure decisions, it is hardly surprising if the rates of tenure rise. This situation serves to underscore the importance of controlling entry to the tenure track. At one of the campuses represented in the Project on Reallocation study, the chief academic officer described in the following paraphrased statement how he controlled entry to the tenure track: *We have approximately 1,060 tenure-track positions and another 1,000 non-tenure-track and part-time faculty. Each year, through resignations and retirement, we have to decide what to do with the vacancies. This discussion takes place with the full understanding that if we fill 40 positions with tenure-track appointments, fully 36 or 37 of the appointees will be tenured at the end of the probationary period. To remain flexible in our staffing, therefore, we have to be very careful about entry to the tenure track.*

Not filling a position when the incumbent vacates not only brings about immediate savings that can be reallocated elsewhere but is probably the least likely of the common ways of reducing the number of faculty positions to arouse significant opposition from faculty, because no continuing faculty member's job is sacrificed. Collapsing positions by attrition, however, impedes the infusion of new ideas from newly hired faculty and the opportunity to realize affirmative action hiring agendas (Mortimer and Tierney 1979; Strohm 1981).

The practice of collapsing vacant positions by attrition probably occurs at most institutions of higher education. The key issues in using it successfully are establishing by formal policy the authority of the institutional administration to review *all* vacated positions and ultimately to decide whether a new appointment should be made, and conducting these reviews expeditiously in the context of a thorough understanding of the needs of the unit for the position as well as the needs of the institution in light of local conditions.

Contract Systems: Institutions without Tenure

Some institutions do not award tenure but typically appoint all faculty to some form of fixed-term contract or rolling contract that can be terminated, with notice, by either party. The most common of these appointments are annual contracts and fixed-term, multiple-year contracts.

Only about 6 percent of respondent four-year colleges and universities in the Project on Reallocation survey had no tenure system. These four-year institutions were overwhelmingly private institutions and predominantly small, less selective liberal arts colleges (Carnegie classification 3.2). According to Project on Reallocation data, about 1 percent of all full-time faculty in four-year colleges and universities were on appointment at institutions without tenure in fall 1981. In 1971, about one-third of both public and private two-year colleges had no tenure system and used some form of contract system (Commission on Academic Tenure 1973; El-Khawas and Furniss 1974).

Such contract arrangements have a number of variations. One interviewee in the Project on Reallocation study described his institution's use of the three-year rolling contract. "Tenured" faculty at this institution are on three-year contracts and are evaluated annually. A negative evaluation triggers a more in-depth review. If the review validates the negative evaluation, the faculty member is sent for counseling and instructional improvement. If, after a second year, the review is still unfavorable, a termination for cause is issued, and the three-year contract is not renewed.

Clearly, the use of fixed-term or rolling contracts to the exclusion of any traditional tenure system and thus the absence of any long-term tenure commitments provide an opportunity for considerable flexibility in staffing. In theory, institutions without tenure that need to reduce expenditures for staffing or reallocate staffing resources can do so just by not renewing contracts. On the basis of case studies of several institutions with no tenure system, one study concluded that contract systems do not provide significant faculty turnover (Chait and Ford 1982). These conclusions are supported in general by the American Council on Education's survey conducted for the Commission on Academic Tenure (1973), which found that about 87 percent of all institutions with contract systems and about 92 percent of four-year institutions with contract systems renewed at least nine of every 10 contracts that expired in 1971 (p. 225). In 1973–74, 93 percent of two- and four-year institutions with contract systems renewed at least nine of every 10 contracts (El-Khawas and Furniss 1974).

The failure of institutions with contract systems to exercise the nonrenewal option has several explanations: (1) unrealized expectations of voluntary attrition as the result of greater faculty career mobility than actually materialized; (2) lack of evidence to support nonrenewal; and (3) the "allure of incrementalism"—that is, the temptation to renew a contract repeatedly to see what additional, conclusive evidence on faculty performance will show up after yet another year (Chait and Ford 1982, pp. 44–46).

Although in practice contract systems seem to be no more effective than tenure systems in stimulating turnover, they do not detract from the real strength of the fixed-term contract: the ability to limit the commitment of institutional resources to a short period of time. That institutional decision makers routinely renew contracts on grounds related to performance does not mean they would continue to do so when a need arises to reduce faculty or to discontinue programs. Compared to institutions with tenure systems, institutions with contract systems can redirect resources more quickly and more efficiently.

. . . the use of contracts to the exclusion of tenure probably is not compatible with the prevailing values at most institutions.

On balance, the use of contracts to the exclusion of tenure probably is not compatible with the prevailing values at most institutions and is not a realistic alternative for most institutions that currently have tenure systems. The effect on faculty morale, the role of faculty in staffing decisions, and the values of academic freedom and economic security would all appear to be called into question by any decision to no longer award tenure but to appoint all new faculty to contracts. Not surprisingly, those four-year institutions that have adopted contract systems have been for the most part new, innovative, and communal and, as a consequence, have had more freedom to implement novel staffing practices (Chait and Ford 1982, p. 14). Furthermore, in censuring one institution using term contracts on grounds unrelated to its contract system, the American Association of University Professors stated that the institution's "term tenure" policy, as implemented, was "fundamentally incompatible with the standards for academic freedom and tenure that are set forth in the 1940 *Statement of Principles"* (AAUP 1979, p. 249, quoted in Chait and Ford 1982, p. 40).

A preferable approach for most institutions is to consider the use of fixed-term, non-tenure-track appointments concurrent with the use of tenure-track appointments.

Non-tenure-track Appointments

Nontenure or extratenure tracks that run parallel to traditional tenure-track systems in the same institution have many of the advantages and disadvantages of term contract systems; however, nontenure tracks appear to be in greater use generally than no-tenure contract systems (AAUP 1978, p. 267). The Project on Reallocation found that in fall 1981, 65 percent of four-year colleges and universities had full-time faculty on non-tenure-track appointments and that about 12 percent of all full-time faculty at four-year colleges and universities (including no-tenure institutions) were on non-tenure-track appointments. On the average, about one full-time faculty member in 12 (8.1 percent) at four-year colleges and universities with tenure systems was on a nontenure track.

The use of nontenure tracks has five advantages for institutions:

1. **Political feasibility:** Unlike conventional term contract systems, nontenure tracks do not replace traditional tenure systems. Faculty resistance to the idea is likely to be less intense than to the idea of abolishing tenure systems.
2. **Absence of AAUP censure:** The AAUP National Convention has yet to censure any institution for using tenure-ineligible appointments when used in addition to tenure tracks. In contrast, both Bloomfield College (New Jersey) and the Virginia community college system were censured when they rescinded traditional tenure policies and introduced term contracts. In a statement published in the *AAUP Bulletin,* the AAUP condemned the creation of a nontenure track as a mechanism to enhance institutional flexibility and denounced the use of the practice as counter to the principles of academic freedom (AAUP 1978). The AAUP recognized, however, the possibility that institutions may need to use non-tenure-track positions to

provide specialized instruction or to meet temporary needs. In such cases, the AAUP recommended that the person and the position be placed on probation and that the use of nontenure tracks be confined to "special appointments clearly limited to a brief association with the institution, and reappointments of retired faculty on special conditions" (p. 270).

3. **Enrichment:** By appointing specialists to fixed-term, non-tenure-track positions, an institution has the opportunity to enrich its curriculum, without long-term staffing commitments, by offering instruction from time to time in unusual or topical subject areas or by hiring recognized practitioners with special expertise in (for example) the arts, government, or scientific fields.

4. **Flexibility:** The opportunity to restrict financial and programmatic commitments is the primary substantive advantage of nontenure tracks and term contracts in general. When institutions are uncertain about student enrollments or student demand for particular course sequences, tenure-ineligible appointments and term contracts provide a means to limit financial exposure and promote flexibility.

5. **Clarity and certainty:** In theory, a terminal or limited-renewal non-tenure-track appointment removes much of the uncertainty and anxiety experienced by faculty on tenure probationary status (Chait and Ford 1982, pp. 80–83).[1]

Just as fixed-term contract systems to the exclusion of tenure appear to be best suited to small, newly founded institutions with a commitment to innovation in curricular and organizational structure, use of nontenure tracks alongside tenure-track positions appears to be suited to the needs of some types of institutions better than others. The

---

1. In practice, however, that case seldom arises because most institutions with a nontenure track allow tenure-ineligible appointees to cross over to the tenure track under exceptional conditions. In a survey of 844 institutions by the College and University Personnel Association (1980), 222 institutions reported providing some "tenure-time credit," usually no more than three years, for service in tenure-ineligible positions.

Project on Reallocation found that among institutions with tenure systems, research universities are significantly more likely to use greater numbers of non-tenure-track appointments than other types of institutions. In that survey, research universities (Carnegie classifications 1.1 and 1.2) had, on the average, 17.6 percent of their full-time faculty on non-tenure-track appointments in fall 1981, nearly twice the average (8.9 percent) for other doctorate-granting institutions (Carnegie classifications 1.3 and 1.4). The average percentage of full-time faculty on nontenure tracks was 7.7 percent at comprehensive colleges and universities (Carnegie classifications 2.1 and 2.2), 7.8 percent at selective liberal arts colleges (Carnegie classification 3.1), and 7 percent at other liberal arts colleges (Carnegie classification 3.2). About 50 percent of liberal arts colleges had no full-time faculty on nontenure tracks. Similarly, about 49 percent of small institutions (less than 1,500 FTE enrollment) and about 45 percent of private institutions had no full-time non-tenure-track faculty.

These differences in the rate of use of non-tenure-track positions by institutional type might relate in part to the larger scale and complexity of research-related activities carried out by research universities (Bagshaw 1984). The use of non-tenure-track appointments allows the research-oriented institution to attract and hire a full-time researcher/scholar with appropriate academic credentials while avoiding the commitment of institutional resources to a tenured position and avoiding the problems of "marginal involvement" associated with part-time personnel described by Leslie, Kellams, and Gunne (1982). The prestige of research universities and their reputation for superior research facilities and stimulating colleagues also may place them in a stronger position in competing for faculty, allowing them to use non-tenure-track positions to attract faculty researchers who would have to be offered a tenure-track appointment at other types of institutions.

The advantages in terms of the additional flexibility gained by limiting resource commitments argue that institutions would do well to consider non-tenure-track appointments in any staffing situation where an academic appointment is called for and the duties of the position clearly require a full-time rather than a part-time appointment but the ability to support the position in the future is uncertain and the centrality of the position to the institution's long-term objectives is questionable.

Part-time Appointments

Beginning in 1976, researchers at the University of Virginia, using surveys of institutions and part-time faculty members, literature searches, and field studies of 18 diverse institutions, set out to describe the parameters of institutional use of part-time faculty in the United States. Leslie, Kellams, and Gunne (1982) summarize the findings of this research, and their work constitutes one of the major sources for this discussion of part-timers.

A part-time appointment is an appointment "for which there is less than a normal range of assigned duties, and the terms of the employment contract recognize the fractional involvement of the worker" (Leslie, Kellams, and Gunne 1982, p. 1). Where the chief advantage of a non-tenure-track appointment is the provision of a full-time academic without a long-term commitment of resources, the chief advantage of a part-time appointment is paying for no more than is needed to have a specific academic function performed.

The primary functions of part-time faculty at almost all institutions are in classroom-related activities (Leslie, Kellams, and Gunne 1982). Twenty-eight percent of all undergraduate instruction and 21 percent of all graduate instruction are provided by part-timers. The pattern of use that emerges in instructional areas suggests to these researchers that part-time faculty are used most heavily in those teaching areas that require flexibility, innovation, and nondisciplinary teaching skills. While part-timers are used heavily in "peripheral, nontraditional, emerging, and low-status" assignments, they are also used in the core areas of programs that require a combination of expertise and experience not found among more traditionally trained full-time faculty (pp. 21–22). In the survey conducted by Leslie, Kellams, and Gunne, 35 percent of institutional respondents reported that the highest percentage of part-timers at their institution were employed as faculty in a business field. The next most frequently mentioned fields were the arts and humanities (pp. 19–20).

Part-timers comprise slightly less than one-third of all resident instruction faculty, and about 210,000 to 215,000 of them are currently employed at American colleges and universities (Leslie, Kellams, and Gunne 1982). Part-timers are used most heavily at two-year colleges and least heavily at major universities. In the fall of 1976, part-timers accounted for more than half of all faculty members at two-year colleges and about 23 percent of faculty members at other higher education institutions (pp. 18–19).

The Project on Reallocation found that in fall 1981 about 93 percent of four-year colleges and universities used part-time faculty. As shown in table 2, about 25 percent of all faculty members employed at four-year colleges and universities in fall 1981 were part-timers.

Using National Science Foundation (NSF) data on employment of part-time faculty in scientific fields, Leslie, Kellams, and Gunne (1982) reported that private institutions are more likely to employ part-timers in scientific fields than are public ones. Slightly more than 24 percent of faculty in scientific fields at private institutions were part-timers in 1976, whereas at public institutions over 17 percent of faculty in scientific fields were part-timers. The Project on Reallocation found that among four-year colleges and universities, private institutions employed significantly more part-time faculty than did public institutions. On the average, about 28 percent of all faculty were part-timers at private institutions, compared with about 20 percent of all faculty at public institutions.

The Project on Reallocation also found that doctorate-granting institutions had, on the average, lower proportions of part-timers in their faculty complement (20.8 percent) than did comprehensive institutions (26.2 percent) and liberal arts colleges (26.6 percent). When these categories are further disaggregated, however, research universities (Carnegie classifications 1.1 and 1.2) had significantly lower proportions of part-time faculty (12.4 percent) than doctorate-granting institutions (Carnegie classifications 1.3 and 1.4) (21.1 percent), and selective liberal arts colleges (Carnegie classification 3.1) had significantly lower proportions of part-time faculty (19 pecent) than less selective liberal arts institutions (Carnegie classification 3.2) (28 percent). The two classes of comprehensive institutions (Carnegie classifications 2.1 and 2.2) had relatively similar proportions of part-time faculty (27 percent and 24.5 percent, respectively).

The use of part-timers was also clearly distinct according to institutional type (Leslie, Kellams, and Gunne 1982). Universities fell into two classes. The first class, which included major, nationally respected research universities, in general used few part-timers and either held their numbers down or worked to decrease the number employed. Particularly in undertaking termination of academic staff, these universities viewed part-time faculty as the most expendable personnel, because they had no contractual security. Their work either was given to full-timers who would otherwise have had light loads or was assigned to teaching assistants. The second class, the large urban universities, used the concentration of professional talent available in their area and relied heavily on part-timers in some fields (pp. 28–29).

The use of part-time faculty in other sectors of higher education appears to depend heavily on the financial and enrollment market conditions affecting the specific institution. A survey of part-time faculty conducted for the AAUP, however, found that the labor market for part-time academic employment is generally a buyer's market, with employing institutions having practically a free hand to determine wages, hours, and conditions of employment (Tuckman and Caldwell 1979).

Two common rationales for employing part-time faculty are economy and flexibility. Many institutions are able to generate many more student credit hours for fewer dollars by employing part-timers (without compensation in the form of benefits) than would be needed if a full-time faculty member assumed the same teaching load (Leslie, Kellams, and Gunne 1982). Thus, use of part-time faculty can yield important short-term savings. This situation is particularly true when programs and budgets are based on the market demand for individual coursework. Salary savings may be less dramatic in other types of institutions, however. A significant factor for institutions employing large numbers of part-timers is the "considerable" administrative expense incurred in hiring and supervising part-timers. Obviously, such costs vary from institution to institution (pp. 2–3).

Increased flexibility in academic staffing, the second rationale for employing part-time faculty, means that institutions are able to avoid long-term commitments to individuals and as a result can easily change course offerings and academic programs to meet market demand. A market model of academic staffing is clearly an inappropriate strategy for some institutions, particularly in areas of study where accreditation by a professional association precludes their extensive use (Leslie, Kellams, and Gunne 1982); however, community colleges, many urban institutions, and a number of private institutions, especially smaller ones where market conditions are of primary importance, should find the use of part-time faculty attractive. Such institutions have little choice but to employ part-timers in large numbers because institutional survival depends on the ability to respond quickly to the local market for educational programs (p. 4).

Part-timers serve as buffers for the full-time staff when enrollments level off or decline (Leslie, Kellams, and Gunne 1982). While full-time tenured faculty can be terminated in the case of a bona fide financial exigency, the typical pattern is to terminate part-timers first. At unionized institutions, collective bargaining agreements often specify that part-time faculty will be the first to go in the event of cutbacks (p. 98). At the same time, full-time faculty tend to be defensive or openly hostile to part-timers (Leslie, Kellams, and Gunne 1982). These findings parallel those of research in business and industry on the attitudes of full-time or unionized workers when confronted with part-time or nonunionized workers (see, for example, Nollen, Eddy, and Martin 1977). Full-time faculty see part-timers as cheap competitors for salary dollars and as threats to status and security. Because most part-timers perform only classroom-related activities, they are able to avoid extensive student contact and advising, as well as involvement in committee work—another source of resentment for full-time faculty (p. 5).

The increased number of part-time faculty is one of the most important changes in the academic professoriate over the last two decades. In 1960, 82,000 part-timers were employed, in 1977, 200,000 (Leslie, Kellams, and Gunne 1982, p. 23). The trend is cause for concern because of one of Leslie and associates' major findings:

It is not at all uncommon for institutions to have no count of part-timers and no way to report on the level of part-time employment. Few institutions have considered part-time employment at the policy level. For the most part, we see a free-wheeling department-level allocation of available faculty slots (p. 143).

Interviews conducted by the Project on Reallocation provide some support for this lack of institutional awareness about its practices relative to part-time faculty. A number of chief academic officers were unable to report accurately how many part-time faculty were employed or how they were being used. A clear implication of these findings is that if institutions are to use the employment of part-time faculty to increase flexibility, they must coordinate and control the hiring of part-time faculty.

Treating part-time faculty employment as a casual departmental affair instead of a central institutional concern is a mistake. . . . Free-wheeling departmental autonomy (with attendant abuses) should be replaced by central responsibility for part-time faculty to insure fair and humane treatment (Gappa 1984a, p. 6).

An institution must deal with several related issues if it is to increase or maintain a substantial number of its faculty as part-timers. First, it must be aware of some of the problems associated with the increased use of part-time faculty. Part-timers may not be as familiar with the college's missions, philosophies, and academic policies as full-time faculty members. It is difficult to meld part-time and full-time faculty into a cohesive college faculty, especially if multiple locations are involved. It is also difficult to coordinate course content, develop uniform standards for students' performance, and establish continuity of instruction when part-time faculty are used extensively (Ernst and McFarlane 1978, pp. 92–97). A major concern for some institutions is the effect of using large numbers of part-time faculty on the scholarly environment outside the classroom. In its report *Involvement in Learning,* the Study Group on the Conditions of Excellence in American Higher Education (1984) recommends that "academic administrators should consolidate as many part-time teaching lines into full-time positions as possible." The group argues that the full-time faculty member is more likely to identify with the institution and become more intensely involved with students, thus contributing to an institutional environment

A number of chief academic officers were unable to report accurately how many part-time faculty were employed . . .

that encourages students' involvement in learning outside the classroom (p. 36). One implication of such concerns is that the competing demands on personnel systems to provide flexibility and to promote learning will require mediation in individual institutions.

Second, the need for qualified part-time faculty should be anticipated and pools of potential applicants established. The goal here is to avoid last-minute scrambles and to engage in some advanced planning concerning adequate compensation in an unfamiliar labor market. A large contingent of part-timers and the specialized matching of their skills to institutional needs may require a full-time administrator (Leslie, Kellams, and Gunne 1982, p. 91).

Third, the compensation for part-timers should be a matter of institutional, not just departmental, review. We stop short of arguing here, as do Leslie and associates, that wage rates should be prorated (p. 91). The wage rates of part-timers should bear some relationship to what the institution pays for instruction as opposed to research and service. Part-timers are often not expected to perform these latter responsibilities.

Fourth, institutions might consider pooling supporting services like secretaries, photocopying, telephone, and so on. In such a plan, departments would be required to purchase services on the basis of full-time enrollment and thereby would spread the supporting workload for part-time faculty. Another concern is providing access to computer facilities for part-timers.

Fifth, an effort should be made to help part-timers become and remain effective instructors. Most faculty development and instructional improvement programs concentrate on the needs of full-time faculty.

Sixth, extensive use of part-time faculty will require the institution to develop an appropriate role in institutional governance for them. The establishment of an administrative position to serve as a focus and conduit for part-timers' grievances would be an effective resolution of this problem (Leslie, Kellams, and Gunne 1982, pp. 91–92). Many part-time faculty, however, express satisfaction with their lack of involvement in governance, and some legitimately need to limit their involvement in committees and collegiate decision making because of full-time jobs elsewhere (Gappa 1984a, p. 5). Certainly, part-timers need a representative of their inter-

ests and an authoritative source for information about their
rights as employees.

Tenure Quotas
A tenure quota places an upper limit on the number or percentage of faculty who may hold tenure at an institution or
in a department at any one time. In 1972, only about 6
percent of all institutions had some form of tenure quota
(Commission on Academic Tenure 1973). Between 1972
and 1974, the proportion of colleges with an upper limit on
tenure levels increased from 5.9 percent to 9.3 percent
(Chait and Ford 1982, p. 120).

The Project on Reallocation found that in 1981–82
almost 30 percent of four-year colleges and universities
with tenure systems had established tenure quotas, about a
third of them at the departmental level. The mean tenure
quota for respondents that supplied a percentage figure was
66 percent; however, responses ranged from 37 percent to
85 percent. The study found no significant relationship
between having a tenure quota and institutional type, public or private control, or other institutional characteristics.

A tenure quota has six advantages:

1. Tenure quotas are *simple* to administer: They focus
   the debate over tenure on determining an appropriate
   percentage rather than on more subtle issues of educational policy and academic philosophy.
2. Tenure quotas promote *flexibility:* When coupled with
   a fixed probationary period, some turnover in tenure-
   track faculty is assured, guaranteeing some influx of
   new blood, new ideas, and the opportunity to respond
   to market changes.
3. Tenure quotas encourage *selectivity:* Tenure committees are inhibited from wholesale acts of collegial gen-
   erosity or charity in granting tenure and cannot avoid
   carefully comparing candidates. Quotas also provide
   weak department chairs, deans, and presidents with a
   useful excuse to be rigorous.
4. Tenure quotas may enhance or restore a measure of
   prestige to the conferment of tenure as a by-product
   of exercising greater selectivity.
5. The turnover provided by quotas can provide occasions to improve or maintain *diversity* in faculty composition by sex, race, and ethnicity.

Flexibility in Academic Staffing

6. Tenure quotas aid in *economical* administration: By ensuring a certain percentage of nontenured faculty, presumably at lower ranks and lower salaries, tenure quotas keep instructional budgets lower (Chait 1976; Chait and Ford 1982).

While these advantages may appear attractive, particularly to leaders of institutions seeking fiscal flexibility, the closer an institution's or a department's actual tenure level approaches the established quota, the more apparent the disadvantages of quotas (Chait and Ford 1982, p. 134).

1. Tenure quotas are inequitable: Only untenured faculty are adversely affected.
2. Tenure quotas may lead to a deemphasis on merit in tenure decisions and a narrow concern with arithmetic considerations, lowering faculty morale.
3. Tenure quotas encourage the transiency that accompanies rapid turnover in probationary faculty, who may experience lower morale, little sense of belonging, and minimal loyalty to institutional values.
4. Tenure quotas tend to engender controversy, and they "can galvanize [faculty] opposition as few other issues can" (Chait and Ford 1982, p. 136).
5. Tenure quotas, when imposed institutionwide, limit the opportunities of institutional decision makers to improve the quality of the faculty. Once the tenure limit in a department has been reached, candidates for tenure who may be stronger candidates than existing tenured faculty cannot be added to the permanent faculty, even though the department may have significant growth potential.
6. The establishment of tenure quotas may disadvantage an institution by making a high level of tenure density legitimate, communicating to faculty and tenure committees that a certain percentage of tenured faculty is normal and that tenure decisions need not be made on strict, substantive grounds until that limit is approached (Chait and Ford 1982, p. 139).

An additional disadvantage can be added to this list: An absolute upper limit on tenure is essentially arbitrary as the "ideal" tenure ratio is likely to change as the composition

The Case of Midwestern College:
Tenure Quota or Rolling Contract?

The question of whether an institution should adopt a tenure quota or some alternative to tenure-track appointments became a source of concern at a midwestern college, one of the case studies for the Project on Reallocation. The board of trustees of the college came to feel that the conditions of environmental uncertainty and the potential enrollment problems resulting from a declining pool of applicants required the college to consider carefully the nature of its commitments. The administration and the board of trustees believed that the college was headed toward what some would call an "overtenured" ratio. The college and the faculty considered a variety of alternatives, among them a tenure quota.

The alternative of a tenure quota proved unpalatable, and eventually the board and the administration proposed to the faculty assembly that every new contract be a rolling contract. Each appointment would be offered initially for three years. Annual evaluations would result in the renewal of the contract for an additional three years; that is, it would require at least two years notice from the institution to terminate the contract.

Although faculty were incensed at the proposal, the compromise eventually worked out between the faculty and the administration was to handle each new appointment individually. The academic vice president brings the projected line and/or position to the faculty affairs committee and proposes that it either be put on the tenure track or become a rolling contract. The rolling contract is often justified, according to the respondent, on the basis of low student demand for the courses being offered. During the two or three years that this system has been in operation, the vice president has proposed approximately half of the new appointments be made rolling contracts. Of a total of approximately 65 faculty, nine were on rolling contracts at the time of the interview. Most of these contracts were in what the college described as low-demand courses in the humanities.

Proponents of the rolling-contract system at the college argue that it gives them considerable flexibility in staffing. If enrollments in the areas affected should drop precipitously, it would be at least theoretically possible to terminate people on rolling contracts with two years notice, and it would not be necessary to declare financial exigency and/or to close a program to do so. Yet the rolling contract encourages faculty members to commit themselves to the college and to participate in college life—at least more than would an annual or part-time employment contract.

of the faculty changes. In some cases, a quota might force an institution to release faculty in high-demand areas—for example, business and computer science—who might be impossible to replace.

In summary, institutions considering the imposition of a tenure quota must answer several questions:

1. What is the appropriate tenure unit(s) against which a quota must be judged—department, school, or campus?
2. What is the likely effect on current tenure-eligible faculty and the nature of the institution's current legal and moral commitment to them?
3. What problem will this quota solve?

Extended Probation and Suspension of "Up-or-Out" Rules
The maximum probationary period for tenure-track faculty at most institutions remains well within the seven-year limit endorsed by the AAUP: 62 percent of the colleges and universities surveyed by the Commission on Academic Tenure in 1972 reported maximum probationary periods of under seven years. The median term was six years for all institutions. In general, private institutions had much longer probationary periods than did public institutions (Commission on Academic Tenure 1973, p. 5). The more recent survey by the American Council on Education shows that the gap between public and private institutions has narrowed and the average probationary period lengthened: In 1978–79, the mean probationary period was 5.7 years at public universities, 6.1 years at private universities, 5.3 years at public four-year colleges, and 5.8 years at private four-year colleges (Atelsek and Gomberg 1980, p. 16).

The use of longer or "extended" probationary periods provides institutions with the opportunity to defer decisions about tenure for a specified period of time. While this delay may present a chance to test the fitness of a tenure candidate over a longer term, this practice does not significantly increase the rigor or improve the quality of tenure decisions (Chait and Ford 1982, pp. 108–9).

Whereas use of extended probationary periods allows an institution to postpone tenure decisions, suspension of the "up-or-out" rule—the policy of granting tenure or terminating the faculty member's employment at the end of the probationary period—allows an institution to delay the awarding of tenure indefinitely. The most common use of the practice occurs in combination with tenure quotas (Chait and Ford 1982). Typically, a "tenurelike" review of a faculty member's performance is conducted in the next-to-last year of the probationary period. At that time, the faculty member is either awarded tenure, denied tenure and terminated, or declared "tenurable." Tenurable faculty are those who would be awarded tenure if a tenured position were available (availability being limited by established tenure quotas). Tenurable faculty may remain at the institution, typically on multiyear contracts, awaiting a tenure vacancy. While in theory tenurable faculty can be terminated at the end of the contract period, in practice it does not seem to occur (Chait and Ford 1982, p. 100). Thus, suspension of the up-or-out rule tends to ameliorate the constraints of tenure quotas.

From the perspective of an untenured faculty member with limited job options, an extended probationary period or suspension of the up-or-out rule may be preferable to the other options of relocation or unemployment (Chait and Ford 1982, p. 109); however, the creation of "tenurable" faculty by suspending the up-or-out rule may be only a cosmetic change that, though politically expedient, masks the true tenure density at an institution. "The straitened circumstances of the 1980s and 1990s may induce both faculty and administrators to support any reasonable policy that increases the probability of tenure and decreases the maximum tenure ratio" (Chait and Ford 1982, p. 111).

The flexibility to be gained by institutions in deferring tenure commitments through extended probationary periods or in delaying the awarding of tenure indefinitely by suspending the "up-or-out" rule will be hard gained, and it is difficult to imagine situations where use of these practices could be considered "reasonable" policies rather than mere expediencies.

In general, alternatives to tenure like tenure quotas, non-tenure-track appointments, and extended probationary periods violate three principles widely supported in the profession and codified in the AAUP 1940 Statement of Principles: (1) that any faculty member with a full-time teaching position should be a candidate for tenure; (2) that probationary periods should be fixed; and (3) that faculty should have continuous employment after completing the probationary period (Di Biase 1979, pp. 172–73).

On the other hand, court decisions have upheld the use of tenure quotas, contrary to the first principle in the preceding paragraph (Di Biase 1979). The courts have not addressed the issue of fixed probationary periods but have upheld an institution's right to have no tenure track and no tenure, which would seem to legitimize indefinite probation. In one court decision (*Abramson* v. *Board of Regents, University of Hawaii,* 548 P.2d 253) in which the plaintiff was denied tenure but continued on annual contracts beyond the probationary period, the court ruled that the contracts stated specifically that employment was for a limited duration. To the extent that this one case sets a precedent, institutions may have no difficulty with the courts in violating the third principle above (Di Biase, 1979, pp. 178–79).

Neither alternatives to tenure nor the courts have altered the classical structure of tenure, and traditional tenure remains firmly in place (Di Biase 1979). Furthermore, the research suggests that alternative staffing practices like tenure quotas and nontenure tracks will withstand legal scrutiny.

The discussions about alternative forms of employment, then, can take place on the merits of an institution's proposal. One has to decide whether fixed probationary periods and continuous employment are good principles for an institution. They are not *required* by a court of law; they are simply characteristics that the AAUP and others have argued constitute good academic practice.

Stricter Standards for Tenure

As an institutional strategy for controlling access to the tenured ranks, the American Association of University Professors supports the gradual application of stricter standards in awarding tenure as an alternative to the use of tenure quotas (AAUP 1977). In light of the changes since the expansion years of the 1960s—declining enrollments, tighter institutional budgets, and high tenure density— cases of institutions' raising promotion and tenure standards "are not isolated instances (Centra 1979, pp. 2, 7).

In the Project on Reallocation survey, the difficulty of attaining tenure was perceived to have increased between 1977 and 1982 at about two-thirds of the tenure-awarding four-year colleges and universities surveyed. About 78 percent of this group of respondents attributed increased difficulty in attaining tenure to more strictly applied criteria for tenure or new, stricter criteria. One respondent characterized the process as one in which tenured individuals had "pulled the ladder up behind them, once they were on board." The most common reasons respondents gave for increased difficulty in attaining tenure were to improve the institution's academic quality and to increase flexibility in academic programs and personnel. (The reader must remember that these data are based on *perceptions* of change in difficulty of attaining tenure, not on actual changes over time in the number or proportion of tenure-eligible faculty awarded tenure.)

Another explanation for tighter tenure standards offered by chief academic officers surveyed by the Project on Reallocation is the existence of more detailed procedures and criteria for review of candidates for both tenure and promotion. Apparently, a great many institutions spent considerable time in the early and middle 1970s developing systems for the evaluation of instruction and defining related criteria for tenure. Respondents reported that faculty committees now *use* these systems and criteria to evaluate candidates critically. In a number of cases, the absence of a terminal degree automatically eliminates the candidate. Other respondents reported that faculty committees are more likely to require candidates to have published books or articles to their credit, even when they are in a teaching-oriented institution.

Perhaps the most obvious example of an institutional policy change designed to make attaining tenure more difficult occurred in a recent collective bargaining agreement in the Pennsylvania state college system. Under the old contract, a faculty member was presumed to be *entitled* to tenure once a brief probationary period had been served. If, after the three-year contractual probationary period was completed, the institution were to deny tenure, it had to assume the burden of proof for showing cause for the denial. Under the new contract, any faculty member up for tenure has the burden of proof to demonstrate his or her fitness. This change has taken place in a system whose tenure ratio is approaching 85 percent.

Finally, chief academic officers interviewed in the Project on Reallocation conveyed a willingness to veto or reverse the judgment of faculty committees more than has historically been the case, at least in the mythology of American higher education. Two lines of reasoning are emerging in these reversals.

First, regardless of the merit of the individual case, the institution does not need another tenured faculty member in that discipline. This line of reasoning has a de facto rather than a de jure effect on tenure quota. One cannot report accurately the number of times it occurs, only that it is now a significant but unmeasured aspect of the tightening of tenure. The second line of reasoning is more likely to occur in collective bargaining if relations between administration and the union are highly adversarial. The argument in this case is that the decision about tenure is essentially one for *management* to make, and, while faculty advice is crucial, ultimately it is still management's decision.

A heightened awareness of managerial responsibility is apparent among chief academic officers, but no empirical information supports its magnitude. Indeed, in light of the perceptual and anecdotal nature of these data, it is possible that more rigorous application of the traditional mechanisms for controlling access to the tenured ranks remains more of a desideratum than an accomplished fact. Few tenure-track faculty are removed before the tenure decision. In 1978–79, for example, only 1,313 of 56,566 tenure-track faculty (slightly more than 2 percent) were terminated before the decision (Atelsek and Gomberg 1980, p. 16). While pruning unlikely probationary faculty from the tenure track will certainly give institutions more flexibility and is consistent with the general approved norms of tenure practice, little hard evidence yet indicates that many institutions are placing a very high priority on this activity.

Review of Tenured Faculty
The extent to which the evaluation of posttenure performance is used as grounds for dismissal is relatively undocumented, but both the 19-campus California state university system and the 14-campus Pennsylvania state college and university system have some form of posttenure

review of faculty (Perry 1983). The implementation of a new tenure policy at Texas Tech University, whereby tenured professors would be reviewed every five years with possible termination for unsatisfactory performance, has drawn national attention (Heller 1984). Chait and Ford (1982), in advocating regular periodic reviews of tenured faculty, note that neither the 1940 Statement of the AAUP nor any subsequent AAUP declaration suggests that evaluation of tenured faculty is inconsistent with the principles of academic tenure. They assume, however, that if performance evaluations were used to dismiss faculty for cause without opportunity for remediation and due process, the AAUP would condemn the process (p. 182). The AAUP has not yet taken an official position on posttenure review, but both the National Education Association and the American Federation of Teachers, while not opposed to performance evaluation for purposes of faculty development, oppose review systems that can be used to revoke a faculty member's tenure (Perry 1983).

Slightly more than half of the four-year colleges and universities with tenure systems in the Project on Reallocation survey reported systematically reviewing all tenured faculty. Less than 7 percent of institutions that conduct posttenure reviews (about 3 percent of total respondent institutions with tenure systems), however, reported that negative reviews were used to terminate tenured faculty.

The apparent reluctance of institutions to use posttenure review for dismissal on grounds of incompetence underscores the relatively privileged position of the individual tenured faculty member when institutions seek to reduce expenditures or reallocate resources. The general pattern of the Project on Reallocation data suggests that most four-year colleges and universities go to considerable lengths to avoid terminating tenured faculty.

Removing tenured faculty as a result of posttenure review has several practical drawbacks for institutions: (1) Institutions do not commonly employ the practice and consequently are likely to encounter the same skepticism and resistance to change that meets any radical innovation in higher education; (2) the practice directly affects the job security of tenured faculty and is likely to be opposed for that reason; (3) dismissal of individual tenured faculty on grounds related to performance will require the institution

Removing tenured faculty as a result of posttenure review has several practical drawbacks for institutions.

to specify and document what constitutes adequate and inadequate performance, provide opportunities for remediation, and observe due process.

A further drawback is the ethical dissonance that may be experienced when posttenure review is carried out with the expressed intent of conducting formative evaluations to enable faculty to improve their performance but evidence of the need to improve performance may be used summatively as grounds for termination. This situation is similar to the one that occurs when academic programs are encouraged to undertake self-assessments to identify areas that will require improvement to upgrade the quality of a program, only to find that the identified areas provide the grounds for budgetary reductions or program closure. In both cases, it is not clear that one process can be used successfully to realize both improvements and reductions.

On the other hand, successful use of the practice may pay off in increased flexibility. On the basis of an extensive mathematical comparison of different methods of lowering tenure ratios, one researcher concludes that any staffing practice that increases the rate of departure of currently tenured faculty members is a faster method of lowering tenure ratios than any of the practices designed to limit the number of faculty who receive tenure or to increase the length of time a tenure-track faculty member spends in probationary status (Vaupel 1981).

Incentives for Early Retirement
An arrangement that provides incentive for early retirement is "any arrangement based on a mutual understanding and agreement between the employee and employer to provide a tangible inducement in the form of a monetary or in kind reward for early retirement" (MacDonald 1980, p. 3). As of 1981, however, although "early retirement may be a much talked about topic in higher education, there is little solid empirical published work on early retirement for academics" (Mitchell 1981, p. 45). In a survey of faculty over age 45 in the Oregon state system of higher education, responses indicated that the three most important conditions that faculty thought would allow them to retire early were additional pay, insurance, and part-time employment (Mitchell 1981). In other studies, larger retirement benefits were the greatest incentive to early retirement, as reported

by faculty, with part-time employment second (Ladd and Lipset 1977; Patton 1976).

Five basic types of early retirement incentives have been identified: (1) early retirement benefit payments that are larger than actuarial tables would justify; (2) lump-sum severance payments; (3) annuity enhancements that increase early retirement income to the amount the employee would have received at normal retirement age; (4) phased retirement or part-time employment; and (5) continuation of fringe benefits (Jenny 1974; Patton 1979, 1983). More than two dozen institutions have early retirement schemes that provide supplements for income lost through early retirement, and recently institutions have made provisions for increases in early retirement annuities to permit or encourage professors to retire before the mandatory age (Patton 1979). On the basis of separate national surveys conducted by TIAA/CREF in 1972, by the University of Virginia in 1972, and by the University of Southern California in 1975, Patton (1979, 1983) reports that a large number of institutions are providing some type of severance payment to bring the early retirement annuity up to what it would have been at the mandatory retirement age (p. 47).

A large number of institutions also offer the option of a reduced work load as an incentive to retire early and as a way to supplement the incomes of those retiring early at reduced benefit rates (Patton 1979, 1983). Some institutions also provide all or partial fringe benefits, including continuing contributions to the pension fund until the mandatory age. A fairly large number of institutions provide supplemental monthly retirement incomes for early retirees. The cost of these incentives can be recovered by not filling vacated positions, by delaying new appointments, or by hiring less expensive replacements (Patton 1983, p. 44). Other incentives reported by institutions in all three surveys include continuing payments into social security, payment of health and life insurance premiums, and payment of pension fund contributions until the mandatory retirement age. In the 1975 USC survey, additional schemes were reported, including lump-sum or installment payment of severance pay; phased retirement through part-time employment; and early retirement supplements to persons retiring at least five years early, calculated so that those retiring earliest received the largest supplements (p. 48).

In one study of nine institutions' use of incentives for early retirement, the most common form of such a program (used at five of the nine universities studied) was phased retirement (MacDonald 1980). At the University of California, for example, a faculty member can agree to switch from a full-time appointment, with no change in tenure status, to a part-time appointment until retirement, which may occur any time up to age 70. Phased retirement at other universities in the study included provisions for accelerating the rate of institutional and individual contributions to the institution's retirement plan. Phased retirement usually leads to smaller salaries and smaller taxes, however (Jenny, Heim, and Hughes 1979, p. 36). The issue for the faculty member is whether he or she can live on a smaller disposable income.

Michigan State was able to reduce the size of its faculty through buyouts and incentives for early retirement (Kreinen 1982). In essence, the plan held out to faculty a number of financial incentives to retire early, resign, or take leaves of absence. The positive incentives were offered, however, in a context laden with negative incentives—the institution's termination of about 100 tenured and eight nontenured, tenure-track faculty. Two-thirds of the terminations were selective, the other third scheduled dismissals in several small academic programs previously targeted for closure.

More recently, faculty and employees at campuses of the State University of New York (SUNY) and faculty and staff at the four-year colleges of the City University of New York (CUNY) who would be at least 55 years old by January 31, 1986, were offered an early retirement option that included a retirement credit bonus for three extra years of employment as the primary incentive. At SUNY, 611 of 2,857 eligible employees (21.4 percent) elected the early retirement option, of whom 452 (74 percent) were faculty members. At CUNY, 750 of 3,200 eligible employees (23.4 percent) took the option, including about 18 percent of the eligible faculty members. Officials in both systems cite budgetary constraints and low turnover rates as causes of "a virtual hiring freeze" in recent years (Ingalls 1985). Although the mass retirement of over one-fifth of those eligible for the option has caused some concern about the loss of key personnel, the flexibility gained by the vacated positions will be used to reallocate staffing resources to reflect demand, to hire younger faculty members, and to realize affirmative action goals (p. 27).

The Project on Reallocation survey found that about one-half of four-year colleges and universities engage in no planning for early retirement with their faculty. Slightly less than 30 percent of surveyed institutions reported having a formal early retirement policy, and slightly more than 20 percent reported negotiating early retirements with individual faculty members informally. On the whole, liberal arts colleges were significantly less likely than doctorate-granting or comprehensive institutions to engage in any form of planning for early retirement. Public institutions were significantly more likely to have formal early retirement policies than were private institutions.

About 35 percent of all institutions surveyed reported providing incentives for faculty to retire early. Of those institutions that provided incentives, about 15 percent reported that they provided supplemental retirement income, about 13 percent offered to continue employee benefits after retirement, about 8 percent offered reduced teaching loads, and about 49 percent offered a combination of these incentives. About 15 percent of institutions that reported providing incentives said they offered "other incentives" for early retirement. Liberal arts colleges were significantly less likely to provide incentives for early retirement than were doctorate-granting and comprehensive institutions. Twenty-three percent of liberal arts colleges reported providing incentives, compared with about 55 percent of doctorate-granting institutions and 45 percent of comprehensive colleges and universities. Public institutions (46.5 percent) were significantly more likely to provide incentives than private institutions (31.4 percent).

Some semantic confusion exists over such terminology as positive and negative incentives, supplements, and modified early retirement. One reason for this confusion is that a number of faculty in public institutions are members of state employment retirement systems (SERS) that have provisions for early retirement with reduced benefits. For example, in the six years from 1974 to 1979, over 60 percent of Penn State's retirements were before the mandatory date. Many of the retirees were employees who were moving to another institution. Retirement benefits in SERS are vested in the individual after 10 years, and it has become customary for those who leave Penn State after 10 years to retire rather than leave their retirement contributions with the state to collect annual interest of only 4 percent. In another Pennsylvania institution, the chief academic officer has been able to encourage some faculty to take early retirement rather than face dismissal. In 1981–82, as a result of negative teaching evaluations, five faculty members, all of whom were at least 55 years of age, retired early when told dismissal proceedings would be instituted. It is clear, then, that early retirements can be part of a lateral move, a career reorientation, or simply an attempt to avoid the unpleasantness involved in fighting a charge of poor teaching.

The findings of the Project on Reallocation suggest that many arrangements for early retirement are individually negotiated. One vice president of personnel interviewed in that study reported that roughly 8 percent of the faculty at the four institutions in his system are on early full or partial retirement, and over half of those arrangements were individually negotiated. He ventured the opinion that the upward limit of such early retirements might be approximately 20 percent of the faculty. At that institution, the program is financed entirely through dollars recovered from the early retirements.

Interviews in the Project on Reallocation study and a review of the literature reveal that public institutions may encounter several legal barriers to the creation of incentive programs for early retirement. In a number of cases, state governments have rules and regulations that prohibit paying salaries and/or remuneration for work not performed.

Providing incentives for faculty to retire early is a short-term strategy for depopulating tenured ranks, a strategy that is not particularly effective as a means of increasing new entry-level appointments in the long run (Hopkins 1972). Moreover, few institutions would want to spend money on a program that causes their most effective teachers and researchers to leave, and most early retirement schemes in both business and academe are therefore intended to encourage marginal employees to leave early (Patton 1979). In a University of California study, salary levels and publication rates were negatively associated with willingness to retire earlier than planned when age and length of service were controlled (Patton 1979).

The actual costs of incentive programs for early retirement are difficult to determine. They depend on local factors as well as such issues as whether early retirees must be replaced, at what rank they must be replaced, and what groups of employees will be given the option to participate. Indeed, the costs may be too high for some institutions. As the 1980s develop, economic considerations may curtail any thought of early retirement on the part of institutions or their faculty (Chait and Ford 1982, p. 233). For institutions with few persons of preretirement age, early retirement incentives make little sense (Patton 1983). Each institution should develop a basic faculty flow model that incorporates historical data on retirement and outmigration rates and policy data on tenure-granting practices, hiring priorities, and other staffing policies like early retirement incentives (Patton 1983, p. 52).

Each institution needs to analyze the extent to which incentives for early retirement constitute an effective way to increase its staffing flexibility and/or lower its costs. These analyses will need to take into account the effects on institutional budgets and planning models of the Age Discrimination in Employment Act, which, as of July 1, 1982, raised the mandatory retirement age in higher education from 65 to 70. The prevailing wisdom now seems to be as follows:

1. In some public systems, incentives for early retirement may be limited as they amount to paying people for not working.
2. The existence of an early retirement option can be useful in helping an institution terminate faculty.
3. Incentives for early retirement can have a "one-time," short-run effect on the composition of the faculty.
4. The design of an appropriate incentive is not easy; in addition to economic considerations, tax implications and potential legal problems must be considered.

Retrenchment

The term "retrenchment" involves some confusion. As used in this monograph and by the Project on Reallocation, it means the dismissal or layoff of tenured faculty members or the dismissal of nontenured faculty members in mid-contract for reasons other than just cause or medical reasons. Of the four bases for terminating tenured faculty considered legitimate by the AAUP—cause, medical reasons, financial exigency, and closure of academic programs—only financial exigency and closure of academic programs are sufficient justification for retrenchment, because just cause and medical reasons are confined to the individual faculty member and the specific circumstances of his or her case.

A survey of the member institutions of the Association of American Colleges at the beginning of the 1970s found that seven of 54 respondent institutions had terminated at least one tenured faculty member for reasons of financial exigency (Gillis 1971, p. 367). In a study of staff reduction policies at 163 public and private institutions in 14 states in the academic years 1971–72 through 1973–74, 74 percent of private four-year institutions, 66 percent of public four-year institutions, and 41 percent of two-year institutions had reduced or were in the process of reducing faculty (Sprenger and Schultz 1974). In 91 of the 163 institutions in the sample, the number of faculty reductions increased substantially each year over the three-year period—from a total of 178 in 1971–72, to 259 in 1972–73, to 517 in 1973–74 (p. 21). Of these 91 institutions, 52 reported declining enrollments as the primary reason for the reductions, with increased operating costs as the second most reported reason.

In a survey of chief executive officers of 300 institutions that were members of the National Association of State Universities and Land-Grant Colleges or members of the American State Colleges and Universities association, 12 institutional respondents reported dismissal of a total 134.5 FTE positions because of financial exigency (Fulkerson 1974).

Slightly more than 16 percent of four-year colleges and universities in the Project on Reallocation survey had retrenched faculty in the five-year period between 1977 and 1982. Ten percent of tenure-granting institutions in the sample had retrenched at least one tenured faculty member during that five-year period. With regard to retrenching faculty, no significant differences were apparent among institutional types or between public and private institutions. Institutions that had experienced declining enroll-

Place
Stamp
Here

Association for the Study of Higher Education
Attention: Subscription Department
One Dupont Circle, Suite 630
Washington, DC 20036

Place
Stamp
Here

ATTN: Serial Acquisitions Dept.
The Library

_____

_____

_____

ment of 5 percent or more over the 10-year period from fall 1972 to fall 1981, however, were significantly more likely to have retrenched faculty between 1977 and 1982 than were institutions that had experienced enrollment gains of 5 percent or more and institutions with relatively stable enrollment (changes in enrollment less than ±5 percent) over the 10-year period.

Three basic questions dominate the national discussion of faculty retrenchment:

1. Under what conditions should (or could) faculty be dismissed or laid off?
2. What procedures are necessary and/or desirable in retrenchment?
3. What criteria should be used?

The argument over conditions tends to revolve around what constitutes bona fide financial emergency and program discontinuance, as virtually all parties agree that faculty may be terminated for cause or for medical reasons. The AAUP advocates a definition of financial exigency that involves a threat to institutional survival that cannot be alleviated by other means, whereas others would adopt a less stringent definition (see Gray 1981 and Hendrickson and Lee 1983 for a discussion of court cases and judicial attitudes on this matter). The courts have defined financial exigency as an existing deficit in an institution's operating budget and have held that legislative reductions in an operating budget constitute a bona fide financial exigency (Hendrickson and Lee 1983). The courts also have held that exigency need not exist in an institution as a whole but can be limited to a single academic unit (pp. 85–86). The unit-specific declaration of exigency might be regarded as suspect in the common situation, however, particularly in state-funded institutions, where budgets are centrally administered and constituent college units are not accounted as self-supporting (Olswang 1983, p. 433).

Discussions with chief academic officers in public institutions and the recent literature lead one to the conclusion that financial emergency is a more useful term than financial exigency. Emergency conveys the relative lack of time to deal with the rapidly changing circumstances involved with revenue shortfalls, while exigency implies general conditions of decline.

The emergency condition of revenue shortfalls is becoming increasingly common in the public sector of American higher education.

Three times in the past 10 years, economic downturns have been severe enough to cause abrupt mid-year curtailments of spending plans in some states, as tax collections dropped with the declining economy. The first substantial cutbacks affecting higher education occurred in the 1974–75 recession, the second in 1979–80, and states face similar circumstances in 1982. (Ten southern states have been affected in the last two years.) (Mingle 1982, p. 1).

The problem in the private sector of higher education is how to address general decline. The most common cases occur when "paid accepts" fall drastically in one year. One chief academic officer lamented in the summer of 1982 that fall enrollment (paid accepts) was going to be 50 students fewer than planned. A $250,000 shortfall in a small college's budget requires some drastic adjustments during the year.

Institutions can take several steps to deal with such emergency conditions (Bowen and Glenny 1976). Briefly, institutions have to consider the advantages of selective as opposed to across-the-board reductions, the limits on flexibility represented by fixed costs, the appropriate student and faculty consultative mechanisms, rules and regulations that limit fiscal flexibility, and procedures for laying off and/or reallocating faculty (pp. 76–77). (For other guidelines to be followed in times of retrenchment, see Fortunato and Waddell 1981 and Melchiori 1982.)

Establishing criteria for retrenchment requires that an institution determine the *relative priority* it places on different institutional areas. The institution has to define:

1. The unit that will be affected by retrenchment (that is, program, department, division, or institution);
2. The categories of personnel (faculty, administrators, or others);
3. The locus of tenure (that is, department, college, or campus);
4. Affirmative action goals; and
5. The order of layoff.

The Closure of Academic Programs

In a time of scarce resources, the discontinuance of some academic programs is an almost inevitable outcome of budget gaps and of such processes as academic program review. The decision whether or not to retain programs that do not meet or are low on specified criteria is an integral part of the entire academic review process. Furthermore, the right of institutions to engage in bona fide program closure is almost unchallenged. The AAUP, for example, accepts it as legitimate grounds for dismissing tenured faculty (Mortimer 1984, p. 62).

Program closure is not *necessarily* a decision to retrench or to dismiss tenured faculty. Indeed, the University of Michigan's policy on discontinuance of academic programs specifically states that the university has never released tenured faculty members because of program closure. Further, if it should become necessary to release tenured faculty within a program to be discontinued, every effort would be made to place tenured faculty and staff in other suitable positions, perhaps through retraining.

It is equally clear that a decision to reduce the faculty or engage in reductions in force need not be a decision to close programs; the maintenance of a program's vitality is often a special goal in guidelines for retrenchment. Several alternatives to program closure have been identified— merger, transfer to another unit, joint programs with another institution, and transferring the program to another institution (Davis and Dougherty 1978).

It is also apparent that substantial technical, bureaucratic, and emotional barriers must be overcome when considering phasing out programs: (1) lack of a data base to interpret criteria; (2) the time-consuming involvement of academic officers, deans, and faculty members; (3) emotionalism and resulting decreased objectivity; (4) distrust by faculty as the result of the failure to consult them; (5) ambivalence over making decisions; and (6) the political climate of the institution and/or state (public and private institutions may vary on this item) (Davis and Dougherty 1978). Closing a program also requires an institution to identify the locus of program authority, the criteria to be used, and the safeguards to be given to faculty, staff, and students.

Program closure is not **necessarily** *a decision to retrench or to dismiss faculty.*

Of the slightly more than 16 percent of four-year colleges and universities that reported retrenching faculty in the Project on Reallocation survey, about half cited program closure, program reductions, and declining enrollment as specific reasons for retrenching faculty. About 13 percent of retrenching institutions gave financial exigency as the primary reason for retrenchments.

Between 1977 and 1982, almost 37 percent of respondent institutions in the Project on Reallocation survey had closed undergraduate programs, another 7 percent had closed graduate programs, and about 16 percent had closed both graduate and undergraduate programs. The mean number of program closures for all institutions that had closed programs was 3.87. Sixty-nine percent of institutions that had closed programs reported that declining enrollment was the primary reason for program closures.

For purposes of discussion, this monograph treats retrenchment as an isolated and fairly limited response to conditions of declining enrollment and financial emergency. Although the AAUP's "institutional survival" test for determining bona fide exigency seems severe, the dismissal of tenured faculty merely to gain additional flexibility may be too cavalier for most institutions to countenance, particularly when other strategies are available. Furthermore, most retrenchments have to be made on projections rather than on actual conditions, and most projections are not accurate enough for this purpose. While the threat of retrenchment or retrenchment notices may spur administrative and academic units to greater efforts to find alternative strategies for coping with reductions, more adequate faculty flow models, enrollment contingency plans, and vital faculty development and retraining programs are more humane solutions. Certainly, the first two alternatives are economically feasible for all institutions.

Finally, a national debate is currently raging about whether program reduction is (or should be) legitimate grounds for dismissing faculty. An institution may argue that it has no intention of closing a history department, it just wants a *smaller* one. The usual method for "downsizing" a department is through attrition, denying tenure, and not renewing part-time or one-year appointments. It is clear, however, that faculty dismissals to reduce programs rather than for reasons of exigency or closure are a growing part of the academic landscape. Dismissals clearly should be used only as a last resort.

Retraining and Reallocating Faculty
Programs for faculty training and development aid in the search for greater institutional flexibility. Retraining faculty in areas of low student demand for reassignment to areas of greater demand makes it possible for some institutions to use some faculty more efficiently.

Four major types of faculty training and development projects have been identified: (1) career assessment and planning; (2) respecialization and retraining; (3) experimental faculty exchanges and internships; and (4) "comprehensive multidimensional projects" (Baldwin 1981, p. 5). Only seven such programs were in operation as of 1981, however, most of them serving primarily a population of advanced graduate students and recent Ph.D.s (p. 67).

A few institutions have encouraged faculty members to retrain so that they could shift to areas of high student demand, and a few institutions have tried to operate midcareer change programs (Patton 1979, p. 21). Interviews with executives in industry, government, and academe found "minimal interest" in midcareer change programs, and an individual organization has little incentive to retrain an employee for another profession, especially when easier, more direct ways to eliminate unneeded employees and acquire needed ones are available (Patton 1979). The majority of career changes in academe have been among faculty who failed to attain tenure (pp. 21–22). More recently, however, declining enrollments and reduced funding have encouraged institutions to look again at midcareer change programs (Patton 1983). Incentives for midcareer change are being used as ways to assist disaffected faculty members to leave academe and to encourage others to leave "so that more drastic measures, such as involuntary termination, pay cuts, and furloughs, can be avoided" (p. 44). Incentives for career changes include variations on paid retraining programs, severance pay, fixed-term earnings supplements, and paid leave to attempt a trial placement in business, government, or another nonprofit setting—with the option to return to the institution at the end of the trial period (pp. 48–49). Like incentive programs for

early retirement, the costs of midcareer change incentives are recovered by not replacing the faculty member, by delaying replacement, or by hiring a less expensive replacement (p. 45).

Retraining programs exist at only a few institutions, and they have been developed principally in situations where the institution seeks to reduce or abolish particular academic programs while maintaining commitments to faculty members in those programs by retraining them for work in fields where student demand is high (Patton 1979, p. 184). Several multicampus systems—among them the state university system of Florida, the Pennsylvania state college and university system, the State University of New York, and the University of Wisconsin—have established retraining programs to "reduce or abolish selected academic programs while maintaining employment commitments to faculty members, . . . [giving] institutions the flexibility to reallocate resources to more productive use" (Patton 1979, p. 25).

Recognizing the declining growth rate of enrollments in the state university system, the Florida Board of Regents authorized $3,000 retraining grants for tenured faculty in departments with declining enrollments to retrain themselves in an area where faculty were in short supply. The grants were to pay for the costs of relocation, tuition, and other expenses of graduate study. Grantees were released from instruction and research for two to four quarters. During the retraining period, the faculty member continued to receive full salary. He or she agreed to return to his or her university to teach for at least one year or to repay the university system one-half his or her salary and the full amount of the grant. In return, the university agreed to find the grantee an appropriate tenured appointment within the system. The program operated from 1974 until 1977.

In the Pennsylvania state college system, the program, begun in 1975, was not limited to tenured faculty, and the retrained faculty member was assured reassignment within the same institution. In 1977, SUNY instituted a program to permit tenured faculty members to retrain in fields more in demand. Selected faculty members typically spend a semester at a state university. He or she receives salary, partial support for books and travel, and a tuition waiver if study is in the SUNY system.

The Wisconsin program was inaugurated in 1974 in response to the possibility of retrenchment. Trainees are provided salary and tuition, and they usually study for two semesters in an in-state institution.

In summary, while career-change programs are appealing in concept, the key question remains whether an institution has an incentive to pay for them when sufficient trained personnel are available in the marketplace and when retrained personnel may take their new expertise elsewhere (Patton 1979, p. 28). Institutions are generally reluctant "to make additional investments in unproductive employees who can be terminated, transferred, or encouraged to retire" (p. 182), but higher tenure ratios, representing long-term commitments to specific individuals who may be retrainable but not easily dismissed, might represent one such incentive.

About 60 percent (1,044) of approximately 1,800 two- and four-year institutions responding to one survey reported that they had an organized program or set of practices for developing faculty (Centra 1977). Another 3 to 4 percent said they were planning such programs. Most of these programs focused on improving teaching skills and conducting research (p. 50). By use of factor analysis, Centra was able to learn about the kinds of programs different types of institutions were likely to employ. Larger colleges and universities tended to rely on sabbaticals and temporary reductions in teaching load. Some smaller colleges used senior teachers or "experts" to train colleagues. Larger two-year institutions relied on staff support specialists in institutional development, audiovisual aids, and other instructional services. Two-year institutions also used a set of practices involving teaching assessment by means of ratings from students, colleagues, and administrators. Faculty members' participation in development programs was generally minimal, and a significant part of the support for such programs came from foundations or government rather than from institutional budgets (Centra 1977, pp. 52–54).

The Project on Reallocation survey found that approximately 58 percent of all four-year colleges and universities have some kind of faculty development program. Only 45 percent of the small institutions (under 1,500 FTE enrollment) report faculty development programs. Among larger institutions, the rate climbs to nearly 70 percent. The proportion of institutions with faculty development programs does not vary significantly with Carnegie classification or type of control (public/private).

The Project on Reallocation also asked institutions whether they have a paid leave program. Overall, 86 percent of the institutions have such programs. The positive response rate was higher among institutions that are part of a multicampus system (93 percent of the institutions that were part of a system offered paid leave), unionized (100 percent), or public (93 percent versus 81 percent for private). Not surprisingly, larger institutions are also more likely to have paid leave programs. While nearly all large campuses have such programs, only 60 to 70 percent of small institutions offer faculty paid leave. In addition to paid leave, 72 percent of respondent institutions report providing other opportunities for preparing faculty for new or revised assignments.

Perhaps the most interesting statistic from the Project on Reallocation in this regard is that only three institutions in the survey (less than 1 percent) reported granting paid leave to faculty to retrain. About 17 percent of respondents reported having faculty retraining for new or revised assignment in 1981–82. The total number of faculty members retraining at those institutions was 103. Doctorate-granting (20 percent) and comprehensive (22.3 percent) institutions were significantly more likely than liberal arts colleges (11.2 percent) to provide faculty retraining, and public institutions (24.6 percent) were more likely than private institutions (13.1 percent) to provide it.

Unionized institutions in the Project on Reallocation study were significantly more likely than nonunionized institutions to provide opportunities for faculty to retrain. About 91 percent of unionized institutions reported providing opportunities for faculty to retrain, compared to about 70 percent of nonunionized institutions. Unionized institutions also were more likely than nonunionized institutions to provide faculty retraining. About 36 percent of unionized institutions provided faculty retraining in 1981–82, compared to about 15 percent of nonunionized institutions.

That unionized institutions are more likely to provide opportunities for faculty to retrain supports the results of one study of collective bargaining contracts, many of which were found to contain language indicating that faculty preferred adoption of alternatives to retrenchment, such as retraining faculty for reassignment (Lozier 1977). Some unionized institutions might have turned to faculty retraining when other alternatives with the potential to lower salary-related costs are not viable because of union opposition (Bagshaw 1984).

Since the early 1970s, faculty development has been synonymous with improving the teaching/learning environment, but its focus on teaching methods has at times overshadowed its other possibilities. Faculty development has had little impact on institutions (Toombs 1983, p. 86), and opportunities and programs for faculty development and renewal are actually waning as colleges and universities face the need to reduce costs (Edgerton 1981, p. 4). Although academics value the substance of faculty development, the evolution and eventual predominance of the view of the college or university as a "managed enterprise" has created a situation in which the welfare and survival of the institution, rather than the welfare and development of its individual inhabitants or components, is the primary impetus to action and focus of attention (Toombs 1983). "Whatever the benefits of this managed institution approach may be, it is not the best climate for thinking about and experimenting with the development of human resources" (pp. 90–91).

As institutions face decreasing flexibility, faculty development can play a role in institutional strategies. The psychological and physiological effects on faculty of the institution's responses to scarce resources and environmental uncertainty (as described in Meléndez and de Guzmán 1983) suggest that the institution's orientation toward faculty development may have to change. In the past, faculty development has subsumed activities such as instructional development, personal development, and organizational development, which have been carried on more or less independently and episodically within institutions. A more productive perspective might be to integrate faculty development activities as one segment of an effective management development plan that involves broad representation and significant participation by faculty members.

The institution that copes successfully with the issues

and problems of the 1980s is likely to have a wide variety of effective management techniques. The topics of this monograph reflect many of these techniques and approaches to institutional management. As the institution develops new approaches to maintaining flexibility in academic staffing, it may consider faculty development as only one useful approach. The institution might also want to involve faculty members more closely in planning, it might consider and evaluate various personnel policies using a faculty flow model, it might institute an early retirement program, or it might turn to new types of contracts and alternatives to tenure. Indeed, it might be time for faculty development to enlarge its focus on the teaching/learning environment as the only crucial aspect of faculty experience and become involved in a campuswide effort to improve flexibility.

FACULTY FLOW MODELS

Campus decision makers face a wide array of policy options as they consider how to maintain or enhance the flexibility of academic staffing. Furthermore, it is difficult to know intuitively how changes in personnel policy will affect the composition of the faculty one or two years in the future, to say nothing of 10 or 15 years ahead. When evaluating policy options, decision makers must use some type of model, either implicit or explicit, to understand the relationships among large numbers of variables, some of which they can control or manipulate and some of which they cannot. Without a model, decision makers can only guess at how their policies will affect academic staffing.

Faculty flow models help in understanding the effects of personnel policy changes. Flow models make explicit the assumptions about relationships among variables that underlie planning analyses. Moreover, faculty flow models describe mathematically the relationships among variables, including demographics of institutional faculty, promotion policy, retirement policy, and long-range staffing goals. Administrators addressing questions about the long-term implications of current policy or the possible effects of new policies might ask, for example:

Without a model, decision makers can only guess at how their policies will affect academic staffing.

- What will the demographics of the faculty look like in five or 10 years?
- How will an early retirement program influence the pattern of new hires of junior faculty?
- Is it possible to decrease the tenure ratio while maintaining promotion policies that make the institution attractive to younger faculty members?

A decision maker can use the model to examine what effects alternative policies have in achieving desired outcomes, to determine which variables exert the largest influence over faculty demographics, and to understand better the probable future makeup of the faculty. Thus, the policy maker can evaluate policy alternatives and at the same time come to understand the problem and the institution's capabilities more fully—what has been called "modeling for insight, not numbers" (Bloomfield and Updegrove 1981a).

While it is possible to make one or two future projections by hand, the use of a computer-based faculty flow model permits the decision maker to explore many such questions in a relatively short time. As computer technology has decreased in price and become easier to use, it has become easier for administrators to explore personnel policies through faculty flow models. The following example illustrates the principles behind many faculty flow models. It simplifies the campus academic personnel structure considerably, but it demonstrates the same fundamentals encountered in more complex models.

Consider a college that classifies faculty members only by their tenure status. Assume that faculty are always hired into nontenured positions and that thereafter they may be reviewed and promoted to tenure. Nontenured faculty also leave the institution through resignations. Tenured faculty members remain tenured until they resign, retire, or die. Figure 1 shows this hypothetical college's personnel system. It is easy to see why the models are called flow models if one imagines faculty members moving from one category to another as their employment status changes.

FIGURE 1
A SIMPLE FACULTY FLOW MODEL

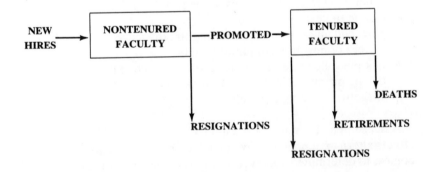

In this model, the number of nontenured faculty each year will equal the number of nontenured faculty last year plus any new hires and minus any faculty members who were promoted to tenure or resigned. The number of tenured faculty will equal the number of tenured faculty last year plus those promoted and minus those who retired, resigned, or died. Historical analysis of faculty behavior can establish the typical proportion of faculty who move from one status to another in a given year. By expressing these relationships in mathematical terms, the administrator can calculate the specific number who will move between the various stages of a faculty career. Such calculations can lead to useful indicators, such as a tenure ratio—for example, the number in the tenured category divided by the total number of faculty members. Even a simple model such as this one can demonstrate that the institution's goals of maintaining a low tenure ratio and increasing faculty productivity (by providing incentives for promotion and maximizing staffing flexibility) will conflict (Hopkins and Massy 1981).

The more advanced faculty flow models follow the same basic principles but add more categories by which to classify faculty and to specify more relationships among the categories. A number of approaches to faculty modeling are available. Most of them are heuristic; that is, they depict the logical relationships among variables but depend on the decision maker to guide the modeling process to a solution. Such models allow the user to explore a number of alternative solutions to a given problem before deciding on the best one. In contrast, some models use an algorithm to find the optimal solution to a given problem; linear programming models are a common example of this approach. Given a number of constraints and goals for problem variables, a linear programming model produces the optimal solution. The basic heuristic models, with examples, are described in the following section.

Types of Flow Models
Markov models
Markov models, named after a Russian mathematician, describe the movements of members of a population through a series of categories or *states,* such as the two stages (nontenured and tenured) in figure 1. Members of the population move between the states according to defined probabilities, aptly termed the *transition probabilities.* A Markov model has two defining characteristics: (1) A finite number of states is involved, and (2) the likelihood of moving from one state to another depends only on the current state, not on what has happened previously. The model has no capacity for any memory of past history. In a

true Markov model, the transition probabilities also remain constant. In some faculty flow models, however, it is useful to change the transition probabilities to reflect how policies may change over time. In either case, by applying the transition probabilities to the number of faculty in each state, the model calculates the number for the states in the next time period. Successive iterations continue the projection for the required number of years.

Like any model, a Markov model needs data to operate, which requires collecting historical data like the number of faculty who fall into each state in the Markov model and the historical probabilities of moving from one state to another. For the institution that has kept complete personnel records, this requirement should not pose a major problem. The transition probabilities can be calculated by examining past changes in faculty status. If, however, recent changes in institutional policy would affect the transition probabilities, such changes must be taken into account. In one study, researchers built a Markov model based on only two years of time series data; while the model proved useful, the researchers recommend more stable data collected over a longer period of time (Spinney and McLaughlin 1979). (See also Hopkins and Massy 1981 and Stokey and Zeckhauser 1978 for more details on the mathematics and technical details of Markov models.)

Stanford University was one of the first institutions to use Markov models to analyze faculty flow (Hopkins and Massy 1981). Hopkins developed a multistate Markov model to evaluate the effects of an early retirement program. The first seven states hold nontenured faculty based on their number of years of service. (Each of the seven states corresponds to one year of a seven-year probationary period.) Six states hold tenured faculty grouped according to age of the faculty member on the basis of five-year age groupings. The last state is retirement. The states were defined in this way because years of service for nontenured personnel and age for tenured faculty were judged to be the greatest determinants of probabilities of promotion, salary, and retirement.

Bloomfield (1977) of Oregon State University expanded on the Stanford model and created a Markov model with 161 states (see table 3). Increasing the number of states permits a more finely detailed analysis, but at the expense of simplicity. In addition, each state must contain enough faculty to ensure statistical validity. With a faculty of approximately 1,300, this requirement did not pose a threat to the validity of the Oregon model.

A more generalized Markov model, the Academic Flow Model, is designed to be readily transferable to other institutions (Bleau 1982). It reduces the number of states to 26 but includes states for part-time and fixed-term appointments. The Academic Flow Model is also more detailed than the Stanford model, because it includes separate states for assistant, associate, and full professors, which are further classified by age. The model was tested and validated at two campuses of the Pennsylvania State University.

Simulators

A second general type of faculty flow model is the computer simulator. While Markov models operate on groups of faculty members according to their state, simulators model faculty cohorts year by year and depend on data on

TABLE 3
DEFINITIONS OF STATES FOR THE OREGON STATE UNIVERSITY COMPREHENSIVE FACULTY FLOW MODEL

Variables	Categories	Number of Categories[a]
Tenure status	Nontenured, tenure	2
Rank	Instructor, assistant professor, associate professor, professor	4
Years in rank	0–3, 4–6, 7–9, 10+	4
Age	0–39, 40–49, 50–59, 60+	4
Years of service	0–3, 4+	2

[a]The combination of all possible values of these variables yields 256 possible states. This total was reduced by deleting states corresponding to nontenured full professors (32 states) and by deleting reference to years of service for tenured faculty (64 states). With the addition of a final absorbing state for separation from the university, this model contains 161 states.

Source: Bloomfield 1977, p. 7.

individual faculty members. The simulator follows faculty members through the various stages of an academic career by using a random number generator to simulate the process of the faculty career. It is a "statistical experiment performed by a computer representation" (Gray 1977, p. 7). For example, each year a certain probability exists that a nontenured faculty member will be promoted to tenure, which depends on a number of factors, including the number of years of probationary service. The simulator "promotes" or denies promotion to faculty based on the values of the random numbers it generates. When applied to an entire faculty, this process comes close to modeling actual behavior. For each year in the projection, the simulator makes similar decisions for every faculty member. The process can vary according to the random numbers used, however, so most simulators run through a given scenario several times and then average the results, giving a more accurate picture of future behavior. The results of the simulated model also show the range of possible outcomes, whereas the Markov model shows only the number of faculty members in each state.

Because simulators operate on data for individual faculty members, they require more data than the Markov models. To use a simulator, an institution must have data such as age, rank, years in service, sex, race, department, and salary for each faculty member. Data on the probabilities of events such as promotion and resignation are also required. Because of the data requirements and the number of calculations and iterations required for each run, simulators are usually limited by the size of an institution's faculty. They are most successful when total faculty numbers no more than 200 to 250. Some larger institutions have used simulators, but they have applied them to schools or colleges rather than to the entire institution. (See Nevison 1980 for a useful and detailed description of a faculty flow simulator.)

A simulator developed at the University of Southern California keeps track of faculty age, rank, salary level, sex, race, year tenured or year of upcoming tenure decision, and department (Bottomley 1978; Gray 1980; Linnell and Bottomley 1975). It would be virtually impossible for a Markov model to keep track of all this information and still be statistically valid because of the number of states it would require. The USC model also requires definition of policies for retirement, tenure, replacement, and promotion. The user must specify, for example, both the probability that faculty members at certain ages will retire and the likelihood of promotion, given rank and years of service. Because of the rich detail of input data, the computer simulator usually produces more complete summaries of the results of modeling. The USC model shows the number of retirements, deaths, resignations, and new positions/vacancies; faculty members who receive and are denied tenure and promotions; and the age, race, and sex characteristics of the faculty—all for the faculty as a whole and for each department. Finally, the model lists the total cost of faculty salaries, average salaries for each rank, and the percentage of total salaries spent on tenured faculty. The output is staggering. (See Linnell and Bottomley 1975 for a sample output of the model.) [2]

Other models

Although it does not quite fit into a category like the Markov models and simulators, EDUCOM's modeling system, EFPM (EDUCOM Financial Planning Model), also deserves mention. Originally based on the highly successful TRADES model at Stanford University (Hopkins and Massy 1981) and built to model financial projections, EFPM is now used to model other college activities, including faculty flow. The modeling system does not fit into a neat category because it is a flexible system that allows users to build context-specific models. Each EFPM model is defined in terms of variables and relationships among the variables. EFPM's work sheet can handle up to 560 variables and 12 time periods and is conceptually similar to the popular electronic spread sheets used on microcomputers. Faculty flow models using EFPM might be designed as Markov models, but other variables are possible as well.

2. The USC faculty planning model is available at small expense to other institutions through Linnell. The user must develop data bases on faculty demographics and institutional policy to use with the model. Because the model is written in BASIC, it is adaptable to the special needs of other institutions. The USC model has had varying degrees of success at large and small, public and private institutions throughout the country (Bottomley 1978).

A number of colleges have used EFPM for faculty flow modeling; Purdue University was one of the first (Knodle et al. 1979). Along with Carnegie-Mellon University, Purdue extended its faculty modeling on EFPM to academic subunits to give more detailed analysis than would be possible at the institutional level. Smith College used EFPM to model faculty distribution by age group and sex in relation to tenure ratios and retirement patterns (Bloomfield and Updegrove 1981b).

In addition to these models, a number of other approaches to faculty modeling in higher education are available. Katz (1977) describes how difference equations can represent a simple model. Schroeder (1974) explains a goal programming model that is more deterministic than the models described here. Bleau (1982) discusses several other less widely used faculty flow models. The majority of institutions that have used faculty modeling extensively, however, have used Markov models or simulators.

Application of the Models

Administrators using a faculty flow model are sometimes looking for a specific answer to a specific policy question—for example, how to assess the effect of current tenure policy on tenure ratios over an extended time period. Spinney and McLaughlin (1979) used a Markov model to analyze six different policies and observed the effect of each on the tenure ratio. Their model showed that the current tenure policy would result in the tenure ratio's rising from 56 to 74 percent and new hires dropping dramatically.

In another case, a Markov model was used to examine a faculty early retirement program at Stanford (Hopkins 1974). Through use of the model, it was discovered that an early retirement program had significant short-term benefits. In the first five years, faculty turnover increased 14 percent. This early gain contrasted to a more modest change over the long term, however, suggesting that while an early retirement program was a solution to an immediate problem in maintaining faculty flexibility at Stanford, it did not offer the institution a continuing solution.

In another application, researchers looked at the effect of affirmative action policies on the male/female ratio among faculty in a program in the natural sciences (Linnell and Gray 1977). They determined that to maintain a level of female employment in the program equal to the rate at which females receive advanced degrees nationally would require 20 percent of new hires be female. Achieving this level was considered difficult at best; thus, the affirmative action goal for the program was redefined in light of the results of the analysis.

Once the broad parameters of a problem are established, successive runs of the model can perform a sensitivity analysis to determine how minor changes in policy can affect outcomes. In completing such analyses, decision makers learn not only the specific answer to one policy question but also which policies have the largest effect on desired outcomes. They can thus begin to develop a deeper understanding of the relationships among many personnel variables. An investigation of changes in cost and tenure ratio as a result of changes in mandatory retirement laws determined that the overwhelming influence on the outcome was the initial characteristics of the faculty group (Bottomley, Linnell, and Marsh 1980). The distributions of age and rank in particular exerted a large influence over changes in cost and tenure ratios.

After a thorough analysis of a number of variables that affect faculty distributions, Eddy and Morrill (1975) concluded that relying on tenure quotas to guide personnel policy is artificial and crude. They found that the whole process of faculty flow depends on and is sensitive to a number of policies. It is highly unlikely that they would have gained this perspective without the model to show them the relationships among policy variables. This analysis serves as an excellent example of how modeling can bring new insight to a problem at the same time it guides policy decisions.

It is important to note, however, that not all modeling analyses lead to new insights or improved policies. After thorough analysis, policy makers at Oregon State University determined that existing policy would permit the institution to maintain academic flexibility. The existing policy, which required that all vacant positions revert to the central administration for reassignment, appeared optimal in this context (Bloomfield 1977). The results of the modeling were "administratively reassuring, although mathematically disappointing" (p. 13).

. . . not all modeling analyses lead to new insights or improved policies.

Experience with the Models

Faculty flow models are one kind of model available to institutional managers. The overall evaluation of the success of the many types of models available to college decision makers has been mixed. In a survey of users of several popular resource allocation models, only 32.4 percent of the respondents felt that the model had met a considerable number of its objectives (Plourde 1976). A more recent survey of users of EFPM found that roughly two-thirds of current users had used the model successfully (Masland 1984). Journal articles suggest that the users of faculty flow models are on the whole satisfied with their models; however, this satisfaction may result from the fact that only those who have been successful have published the results of their efforts. Because model builders are frequently the prime users of faculty flow models, the perception of success may be further biased. It is likely, however, that flow models are more successful than other models because they are not terribly complicated and are easy for decision makers to understand and use. Participants in Harvard's Institute for Educational Management have used a faculty simulator in a personnel course for several years. These top-level administrators found the model easy to use and to understand (Chait and Ford 1982).

The use of certain principles can improve the chances of success for those who want to use the models. They fall into two broad categories: (1) the technical issues of building and using a model, and (2) the organizational issues related to successful implementation of the model (Masland 1983).

Without accurate and complete data, no model is useful. But a serious lack of data is a common technical problem in modeling (Johnstone 1974). In an area such as faculty flow, most institutions have the basic data in personnel files or can obtain the data directly from faculty members. If information on transition probabilities, for example, is not available, the rudiments of a data base can be collected over a two-year period. Modelers can then validate the initial estimates of the transition probabilities during the following years. Even if data are available, however, decision makers should validate a model by checking its predictions against actual future trends. Validation can correct any gross errors and fine tune the probabilities.

Modelers may build too complicated a model: Modeling should start simple and stay simple (Hammond 1974). A simple model can be quite informative and helpful, demonstrating policy changes and the relationships among variables. A more complicated model may confuse the issues and solutions.

A successful model should adapt easily to changing situations on the campus and in the college's external environment. It should be a simple matter to change personnel policy variables and to observe their effect on faculty. Most top administrators, for example, will not want to have to change transition probabilities directly in a Markov model and will be more likely to use the model if it asks them straightforward questions about the chances of moving from one state to another. For those considering purchase of a model from another institution or consultant, the critical question is whether the model is flexible enough to meet the specific needs of the campus. Many models that look flexible may not be able to incorporate all of an institution's idiosyncrasies.

Although technical problems continue to arise, modelers have learned from their mistakes of the past 15 years. The ability to build useful models has also benefited from changes in computer technology. Thus, in today's institution technical problems may be less of a stumbling block than organizational issues. No model is valuable if the people who should use it do not do so. To increase the chances of success, the faculty flow model should be believable; the output and recommendations it produces should make sense to its users. The model's results should be relevant to the problem at hand so that useful information is available to policy makers. And the information must be in a format that communicates the important information and variables clearly (Morisseau 1973).

It is equally important that modeling have the support of top administrators on the campus. Without support, efforts at modeling will flounder. But, particularly for a faculty flow model, top management's support is not the only necessary factor. Faculty members themselves must understand the model and trust it. The faculty will be more apt to accept policy changes based on modeling if they are comfortable with the model and how it is used. In fact, using a flow model in a joint administrative and faculty committee so all concerned parties can participate might be beneficial (Linnell and Bottomley 1975).

Faculty flow models can be helpful tools for understanding the relationships among personnel policies and faculty demographics. Use of models can enhance knowledge of the interactions of important variables and can help the user evaluate alternatives before policies are changed. A number of approaches to flow models are available. The administrator interested in exploring them further should examine the institution's needs carefully. For large institutions, a Markov model is probably the best approach. For smaller colleges or subunits within a larger institution, the simulator may provide additional, useful details. Because the literature on flow models describes several approaches, an administrator or faculty member with basic computer skills may be able to build his or her own model, using microcomputer software such as Visi-Calc or similar programs. Groups like EDUCOM are also available to help colleges and universities with modeling.

This discussion must conclude with a caveat. Although a flow model can show the effects of any early retirement program or the imposition of a tenure quota, none of the models described can answer the more important questions of how to evaluate faculty for promotion, how to make individual decisions about awarding tenure, how to best maintain the faculty's vitality, or whether the faculty in one discipline should be expanded at the expense of another. The decision maker must use sound judgment and experience to answer these questions.

REALLOCATION AND REDUCTION STRATEGIES

The study of the use of faculty staffing practices and institutional efforts to reduce expenditures and reallocate resources has resulted in a typology of reduction and reallocation strategies (see Mortimer and Taylor 1984). The following section identifies these strategies and makes a number of observations about their effectiveness. In some cases, the observations lend themselves to recommendations for effective practice; in other cases, they simply express dilemmas inherent in their use.

The Strategies

For heuristic purposes, two approaches to reduction and reallocation and two ways to implement those approaches are identified. A two-by-two matrix is the result (see figure 2).

FIGURE 2
INSTITUTIONAL APPROACHES TO REALLOCATION

		Management Strategy	
		Attrition	*Decrements (Increments)*
Type of Implementation	*Across-the-board*	Laissez-faire Management	Traditional Planning
	Selective	Starve Problems/ Feed Opportunities	Strategic Planning

Attrition is probably the more common approach to reallocation. In this situation, institutions merely capture loose positions and funds as they become available. It is essentially a reactive strategy. On the other hand, some institutions plan decrements to handle decline. This approach is a more aggressive institutional strategy and involves the preparation of plans and contingencies to handle decline over three to five years. The two approaches to reallocation, attrition and/or decrements, can be implemented across the board or selectively. Four specific management strategies therefore result.

Across-the-board attrition is reflected when expenditures are reduced by not replacing personnel who resign or retire, deferring building maintenance, or failing to replenish depleted stores of supplies. In these situations, the institution may administer hiring and spending freezes

---

indiscriminately to all academic units. Across-the-board attrition is seen frequently in colleges and universities in the first few years of financial shortfalls and/or distress (Bowen and Glenny 1981; Dickmeyer 1983).

Across-the-board decrements occur when all budgets or certain items in them are cut by some percentage. In this situation, travel, maintenance, and equipment purchases are particular "targets of opportunity" for decremental funding. Across-the-board decrements are a common response to financial stress (Mortimer and Taylor 1984).

Attrition and decremental approaches to reallocation and reduction can also be administered selectively. *Selective attrition,* characterized as "starving the problems and feeding the opportunities" (SPFO), allows slow budget reductions or reallocation of resources from marginal or low-priority activities to areas of strength and high priority. Institutions that exercise central control over vacant positions, for example, may decide not to replace a retiring history professor, while authorizing a business administration department to hire additional faculty.

Selective decrements, which are typified by the current interest in strategic planning, occur in at least three different ways:

- The imposition of standard budget targets on each of the institution's units and the reallocation of funds to high-priority programs;
- The imposition of variable targets to create a reallocation fund (a fund for excellence?);
- Reallocations that arise from and follow priorities that have been identified through a comprehensive program review process.

These four strategies or approaches to reduction and reallocation demonstrate the subtleties of managing academic affairs. Each academic unit can be dealt with as a problem or an opportunity, or as a high or low priority, or in decremental/incremental ways.

The matter is further complicated by the context of the institution itself, however.

In the early stages of decline, institutional actions are highly political; above all they seem to be aimed at keep-

ing interest group reactivity at a low level. However, as fiscal conditions worsen, more traditionally rational approaches begin to appear and, by the time the crisis truly arrives, rational strategies of high reactivity are commonplace. It seems clear that highly rational reactive strategies become politically feasible when conditions become desperate, but not much before (Leslie 1984, p. 94).

While Leslie's reference is to fiscal management, the implications for those in academic personnel are consistent with his observations and our values. Options for retrenchment become viable only after almost everything else has failed or when not enough time is available for other options to be implemented.

Effectiveness of the Strategies

The nine observations concerning the effectiveness of the four reduction and reallocation strategies cluster around three major headings. The first three points have to do with the context of budget cuts and their effect on institutional politics. The next five points relate to the strengths and weaknesses of the various strategies for reduction and reallocation. The ninth point is a comment on consultation processes in reallocation.

1. *Both academic and nonacademic areas feel the effects of reallocating resources.*

One large university reported that it had reallocated some $25 million over an eight-year period. Although $10 million of that amount had come from academic areas, $22 million of the $25 million went to pay energy-related bills. One-third of the chief academic officers responding to the Project on Reallocation survey reported that money had been allocated into academic affairs from other areas during the last three to five years. Forty-seven percent reported no change, and 17 percent reported they had lost money to other areas within the institution.

2. *Budget cuts and reallocation put great pressure on existing formulas and traditional systems of allocating resources.*

An example of such pressure occurs in institutions using decremental strategies. It is very difficult to hand out budget cuts based on *anticipated* enrollment declines and/or budgetary shortfalls. For most institutions, projecting enrollments for individual academic units tends to be an art rather than a science. It becomes a guessing game to hand out internal budgetary cuts based on *projected* enrollment declines in academic units unless enrollments are capped as a matter of strategic priority rather than as predictions of student demand.

Further, the more complex the institution, the more difficult it is to establish direct links between enrollments and size of academic staff. Faculty and administrators at complex universities argue that teaching is only one of the duties of a faculty member. Research and service may be regarded as equal or more important, and reduced enrollments can be seen as opportunities to increase effort in the other areas. In response to such arguments, some institutions have begun to consider such activities as continuing education as a part of normal course loads rather than extra compensation.

3. *It is difficult to persuade those in low-priority areas that they should be low priorities.*

Those who are losing funds and/or resources seldom think it fair or wise. Most deans of education, for example, are committed to helping the school of education and believe it is lack of wisdom that causes campus administrators to cut their budgets or collapse positions merely because enrollments are waning. On the other hand, because the major share of the reallocated money goes to pay the hidden costs of energy and fringe benefits, those who are identified as high priorities want to know where all the money went! It is hard to reallocate funds fast enough to handle the enrollment shifts that occur when students change their preferences. Built-in rigidities in the faculty personnel system, for example, work against rapid deployment of faculty resources into areas that experience marked gains in enrollment over a short period of time (two to three years).

4. *Decremental budgets and planning systems help focus attention on priorities, but they are very difficult to implement over time.*

In one university, each academic unit was put on a five-year decremental target. The average target was 7 percent, but the range was from 0 to approximately 15 percent. Planning documents had to be filed to show how each of approximately 12 academic units intended to meet its five-year target.

Some very good results emerged from the targets:

- Over time, the university community learned to believe that budget shortfalls were a reality.
- Some academic officers began to think of how to raise money instead of just how to spend it!
- Debate arising from the decremental targets identified at least 14 major policy dilemmas for universitywide rather than college-level decisions (for example, management of enrollments, academic and administrative computing resources, and funding for libraries).
- Over time, some academic offices began to implement vertical as well as horizontal cuts.

To be effective over time, however, such systems need to be able to accommodate contingencies, such as changing assumptions and projections on which the targets were based. In one case, a college did not actually experience the enrollment declines that were *expected* when the targets were handed out. In another case, an abnormal number of faculty retirements, resignations, and tenure denials resulted in greater flexibility in the unit than had been anticipated when the targets were specified.

5. *Leadership of the highest order is required to establish the point that setting priorities among academic units is the responsibility of the next highest level of decision making.*

One of the major internal debates about reallocation is the relative authority of various levels in the decision-making structure. Private institutions that operate on fiscal philosophies of "every tub on its own bottom" have to resolve the dilemma of how much of the total institutional revenue belongs to the institution as opposed to the sub-unit that generates it. One private university has decided that it would use most of its income from annual giving to "subsidize" the liberal arts college. The professional schools are supposed to be on a break-even basis. Public institutions that get state funds based on a formula find it difficult to reallocate internal funds on some method other than the formula.

6. *An effective strategy of starving problems and feeding opportunities requires a reasonably consistent definition of the problems and opportunities.*

At most institutions, less than 3 percent of the budget is available for reallocation in any one year. It therefore takes three to five years before the SPFO strategy has any significant effects. Administrators have to be careful that the effect of reallocation and/or reduction is in a consistent direction. The effectiveness of selective attrition is compromised when the leadership of the institution and/or the academic units involved change significantly, because such changes often require the reexamination of priorities. In cases where priorities vary substantially from year to year, the net effect of SPFO over five years may be zero!

7. *The key of success in most systems of strategic choice is realistic expectations.*

Since reallocation devices operate largely on the margins of resource allocation, a danger exists that those systems will overpromise the results that are likely to occur. As long as institutions continue the overwhelming, historical pattern of allocating resources based on gradual *incremental* or *decremental* patterns, one can reasonably be skeptical of devices that promise to make such historical truths. On the other hand, some institutions that have encountered severe external crises, such as financial exigency, budgetary shortfalls derived from declining state appropriations, or significant economic downturns in the environment, have been able to accomplish a significant amount of reallocation through SPFO and strategic planning.

8. *Administrative reorganizations and program closures do not save significant dollars in the short run, unless positions are eliminated.*

As most of the cost of a program is in the people used to staff it, saving costs without eliminating positions is unlikely. On the other hand, effective management of program closures and reorganizations may save funds over the long run through attrition or through cost-avoidance techniques. Institutions may choose to close programs rather than to spend the funds that would be required to significantly upgrade them.

9. *Faculty committees work best when they are not asked about individual programs or people but about methods and criteria.*

The ethic of the academic community requires that faculty be consulted about such important decisions as creating, reducing, and closing programs and about reallocation plans. Many faculty refuse to participate in the identification of specific colleagues to be terminated, for example. In some cases, faculty are willing to participate in the identification of programs to be closed, but only after extensive debate about the method, process, and criteria to be used to arrive at such judgments.

Several examples illustrate this point. In a small liberal arts college, the chief academic officer provided information and an analysis to a faculty committee. The committee eventually supported his judgment that closures and/or terminations were necessary, but it refused to identify the specific individuals of programs to be terminated. Yet the legitimacy and trust gained through this extensive consultation was a crucial ingredient in maintaining stability on campus during the terminations. In another case, a standing committee of the faculty senate, the layoff committee, was successful in persuading the administration that layoffs were not necessary if certain other reallocation policies and practices were adopted. This faculty committee was very active in persuading colleagues in departments around the university to get their teaching loads and student/faculty ratios more in line with the universitywide criteria. In still another case, a university created a budget panel consisting of administrators and faculty. The panel advises the administration annually concerning allocating resources. This normal budgetary allocation device is a significant factor in identifying programs and units that can be targets of opportunity in times of decline, and the pattern of regular consultation is a significant factor in the identification of areas for potential budgetary cuts or reallocation.

CONCLUSIONS AND RECOMMENDATIONS

The changing context of higher education requires institutions to recapture some measure of flexibility. This monograph has sought to provide a comprehensive description of major staffing practices that have the potential to increase flexibility and has discussed some of the principal issues involved in their use. Although the definitive study of how institutions learn has yet to be written, the practical wisdom of most administrators would suggest that reasoning by analogy to the experience of other "exemplar" and "sister" institutions—those perceived as similar to one's own—plays an important part in institutional decision making.

The term "flexibility" has enjoyed considerable currency in a number of recent contexts. The term has been used here to signify the degree to which managers of institutional resources have alternatives to allocate or reallocate academic resources, whether in the form of funds or positions. Flexibility ameliorates the problem of declining resources by allowing institutions greater choice in the areas where expenditures need to be reduced; flexibility buffers critical institutional functions from the impact of environmental turbulence and uncertainty by providing options for redirecting resources.

Although this monograph advocates the creation of greater flexibility through academic staffing practices, it does not suggest that any particular practice is a panacea with immediate restorative powers. Not every institution has experienced scarcity and uncertainty to the same degree or in the same way, and the usefulness of each practice examined in this work depends on the context in which it is used. Most institutional efforts to achieve flexibility will not be rewarded overnight but will accrue undramatically, by small increments, over a period of time. For institutions that need to retrench in the short run, this point may mean flexibility will be used as soon as it is acquired.

It is not the intent of this paper to equate institutional flexibility with autonomy or license in making decisions about personnel matters. Institutions should be held accountable in their expenditures of funds and their management of human beings, and they should conform to accepted standards of governance like adequate consultation with faculty in decisions about staffing policy. Within reasonable limits, fiscal constraints are appropriate, and most institutions can increase their flexibility within the bounds of traditional frameworks for governance. The research suggests, for example, that many institutions do not pay sufficient attention to entry to the tenure tracks. The decision to renew or create a tenure-track position and the search for the best person to fill it are matters of some importance to the institution and should be accorded more attention at the institutional level than often occurs. (See Waggaman 1983 for a discussion of the articulation of institutional and departmental needs in recruiting and appointing faculty.) Similarly, institutions frequently have no policies governing employment of part-time faculty and little reliable information about the number and distribution of part-timers employed by their academic departments (Leslie, Kellams, and Gunne 1982). Thus, in the areas of admission to the tenure track and part-time appointments, significant sources of flexibility may exist.

This final section recommends the adoption of a contingency perspective in developing an institutional staffing strategy on the grounds that the effectiveness of each practice depends almost entirely on context. An effective institutional strategy must be based not only on a realistic assessment of environmental forces and their impact on the specific institution (Keller 1983) but also on a realistic assessment of the institution's potentialities. The recommendation of a contingency perspective leads to nine additional recommendations for developing a coherent staffing strategy for the individual institution.

Develop an Appropriate and Comprehensive Institutional Strategy

Not all institutions are facing the prospect of declining resources, and among those that are, the type and degree of declining resources vary widely. Because institutions differ and do not face the same resource environment, no single strategy is appropriate to all institutions. Each institution should determine its own staffing strategy based on its academic and fiscal priorities, its current faculty mix, and its assessment of relevant environmental factors. The determination of this strategy will require knowledgeable answers to the questions raised earlier in this monograph about use of each staffing practice. In most cases, developing a staffing strategy will require institutions to take a three- to five-year perspective on staffing demographics and to consider whether any one of the several faculty flow models is appropriate.

Know Your Institution

Good management results from *informed* choice. To assess the effect that environmental factors are likely to have on an institution, whether as constraints or as opportunities, an institution's management requires detailed knowledge of the institution as well as its environment. Detailed knowledge is also needed to assess the relative costs and benefits of changes in the type or extent of staffing practices used.

Those familiar with the literature on academic planning will recognize the importance of a data base in making decisions that affect institutional vitality. Information about personnel, about academic and fiscal policies, and about practices should be linked in a data base that encourages analytical thinking. One chief academic officer interviewed for the Project on Reallocation described his institution's attempts to develop links between the three areas as follows: *First, we try very hard to identify and establish our priorities. Second, we are very careful to know where our slack—in terms of people and resources—is located. Finally, we make decisions that are designed to match our priorities with our slack.*

Know What Your Institution Values

Establishing priorities and developing an appropriate institutional strategy require an identifiable set of institutional values. Some readers may be uncomfortable with the attribution of a value system to a nonhuman entity; nonetheless, those with responsibility for the overall functioning and direction of the institution—institutional managers—put institutional values into effect through their decisions on behalf of the institution. These managerial decisions are not based solely on the personal value systems that particular individuals bring to the role of institutional manager but are shaped by socialization processes and by the context of formal and informal statements of institutional mission, goals, and policies that have been established over time. Institutional values are thus the purposive content of this received body of institutional goal statements as interpreted and enacted by institutional managers.

Establishing priorities and developing an appropriate institutional strategy requires an identifiable set of institutional values.

The process of managerial vision and revision of what is valued in light of new circumstances leads to different institutional strategies. Some institutions "merely intensify their efforts in regard to their primary mission, a few change radically, but most, either inadvertently or deliberately, redefine their mission . . . by what they choose to eliminate; by reallocation of priorities; by conscious choice; or by state-level mandates" (Peterson 1984, p. 42). Each initiative may represent appropriate institutional strategies when based on knowledgeable assessments of an institution and its environment.

Temper Expectations (and Aspirations) with Realism
No single staffing policy or practice is capable of remaking an institution or providing unlimited degrees of flexibility. For the most part, institutional efforts to achieve greater flexibility through changes in staffing practices will be rewarded undramatically, by small increments, over a period of time. For many institutions, flexibility to be gained by staffing innovations will accrue "on the margins," while traditional staffing practices remain the central feature of personnel policy.

A mix of carefully chosen practices will serve most institutions better than investment in the one practice that appears to have the highest or most immediate payoff for the institution or a blanket commitment to all practices that hold some promise for freeing resources. While a shotgun approach in the quest for flexibility is not the solution, institutions should examine each practice and develop policies for their use (and nonuse) in light of their own conditions. Every institution should know why it uses the mix of staffing practices that it does and under what circumstances it should consider changing the mix.

Not only expectations but aspirations need to be realistic. A tendency sometimes exists for those advocating an innovation to sell the idea by overpromising the results. Staffing innovations that result in greater flexibility will provide opportunities for qualitative growth, but, even when successfully implemented over a long period, they are unlikely to significantly improve the institution's academic reputation.

Link Personnel and Fiscal Affairs

An essential ingredient in any personnel policy is cost, and implementing the staffing practices described earlier involves both opportunity and carrying costs. The actual costs of incentive early retirement and faculty retraining programs are difficult to determine in the abstract but will depend on such diverse factors as the condition of the economy, state laws governing faculty employment, faculty attitudes toward their work and toward retirement, the degree of professionalization and specialization of faculty, whether retirees and retrainees must be replaced and at what rank, and local market conditions (Chait and Ford 1982; Mitchell 1981; Patton 1979). The costs of these programs simply may be too high for some institutions. As noted earlier, about 50 percent of four-year colleges and universities in the Project on Reallocation survey engaged in no early retirement planning with faculty, and about 20 percent informally negotiated early retirements with individual faculty. About 17 percent of survey respondents reported faculty retraining in 1981–82.

While use of part-time faculty, non-tenure-track appointments, or fixed-term contracts may generate considerable flexibility in the form of salary and benefits savings for reallocation and reduced tenure commitments, considerable administrative costs may be involved in hiring, supervising, and evaluating the performance of such personnel (Chait and Ford 1982; Leslie, Kellams, and Gunne 1982). In some cases, extensive use of part-timers may jeopardize the accreditation of programs by professional associations.

Match Solutions to the Problem

Use of part-time faculty is by far the most prevalent staffing alternative to traditional tenure-track staffing at four-year colleges and universities. About 93 percent of institutions in the Project on Reallocation survey used part-timers, rivaling tenure itself as a widely used staffing practice. About 65 percent of institutions with tenure systems also used full-time, non-tenure-track appointments. The political costs to institutions of using alternatives to tenure-track staffing can be reduced substantially by confining staffing solutions to the vicinity of staffing problems. A part-time appointment is clearly appropriate when the staffing problem is that an academic appointment is called for and the responsibilities of the position are less than what would be required for a full-time faculty member. A non-tenure-track appointment is clearly appropriate when the staffing problem is that a full-time academic appointment is required but the ability to support the position in the future is uncertain and the centrality of the position to the institution's long-term objectives is questionable.

Less clear, particularly to faculty colleagues, is the appropriateness of situations in which several part-timers take over the responsibilities previously handled by one tenured faculty member, or when all new hires in a department are appointed to a nontenure track. Institutional resource managers need to keep in mind that while practices like part-time and non-tenure-track appointments promote flexibility, flexibility is neither an end in itself nor sufficient justification to use such practices indiscriminately.

Manage Entry to the Tenure Track

On the basis of research conducted for the Project on Reallocation, one staffing area where many institutions can increase their flexibility while minimizing the attendant economic and political costs is the tenure track. The decision to renew or create a tenure-track position, the search for the best qualified person to fill the position, and the decision to award tenure to a probationary faculty member are matters of some importance to the institution and should be accorded greater attention by institutional managers. This monograph stops short of endorsing Centra's (1979) conclusion that because of changes since the expansion years of the 1960s—declining enrollments, tighter budgets, and higher tenure density—college and university faculty must now *prove* that they deserve tenure. The issue instead is that, because of constraints, many institutions will be able to afford to fill as tenure-track appointments *only* those positions that are central to the identity and viability of the program and the institution; to appoint, after a thorough and objective search, only the *most* promising applicants; and to award tenure and promotion only to the *most* deserving candidates, with the recognition that these awards have been made at the expense of forgoing something else of value. This recognition argues for greater attention to communicating institutional constraints and expectations clearly to search committees when granting approval to fill a tenure-track vacancy and to assisting promotion and tenure committees to understand the bases of the institution's direction and commitments in personnel matters.

Manage Positions, Develop People
In a complex, nonprofit, goal-ambiguous, professionally oriented, labor-intensive organization, people are the most precious asset. In times of rapid growth, higher education recruited large numbers of people, often indiscriminately. In times of stable or scarce resources, people need to be recruited selectively and dismissed humanely. Institutions need to show at least as much concern for those who will stay as for those who will leave, however (Peterson 1984). Faculty who will remain at the institution need to be reassured when they are clearly not at risk, and the best reassurance is to involve them in the institution's planning. This monograph suggested earlier some specific ways to accomplish this feat. Ensuring adequate consultation with faculty generally involves six elements:

> *Consultation should occur early in the decision-making process; the procedures for consultation should be uniform and fair to all parties; there must be adequate time to formulate a response to the request for consultation; information relevant to the decision should be freely available; the advice rendered must be adequately considered and feedback given; and the decision, when made, should be communicated to the consulting group* (Mortimer and McConnell 1978, p. 275).

It is not enough to simply manage human resources as an indirect result of managing positions and programs; human resources must be *developed*.

Institutions can provide a number of low-cost/high-payoff nonmonetary rewards to sustain successful faculty:

> *. . . new faculty slots to build a critical mass of colleagues; authorization for a new course, program, or degree; research assistants; teaching assistants; more clerical support; additional laboratory or computer equipment; an increased library budget; a reduced course load; smaller (or larger) classes; better students;*

a more compact schedule; a sabbatical; travel funds, research funds, or funds for a colloquium; and additional space for an honors or tutorial program. Any and all of these "payoffs" create conditions conducive to effective performance . . . (Chait and Ford 1982, p. 209).

The gesture of thanks for a job well done may be as important as the absolute amount of money involved.

Preserve Managerial Prerogatives by Exercising Them
Different sections of this monograph have focused on different facets of a single theme: Institutional managers need to make informed choices in guiding their institutions through uncertainty. To some extent, uncertainty is a given, although examining the local context in one's assessment of actual conditions at a specific institution is important. For the most part, this monograph has dwelt on ways that institutions can increase their options through various staffing practices that promote flexibility. It has also stressed the importance of informed choice, both by describing the extent to which these practices are in use nationally and by arguing for more comprehensive institutional data bases that link faculty demographic and fiscal information.

The simple fact remains that institutional managers do indeed need to choose. The analysis of institutional data will provide a clear picture of constraints on resources and opportunities to use them, and the process of consultation will provide a variety of views about what the priorities governing the allocation of institutional resources should be. Only those charged with the management of the institution, however, have the authority to decide what the priorities are and what policies will be formed to underwrite them. When this authority is not exercised, or when it is exercised in a way that appears weak, arbitrary, or capricious, the institution may drift aimlessly, act at cross-purposes, and be subjected to considerable internal and external strife until decision-making power finds its way to other, and possibly more callous, hands.

"If decision makers cannot say 'no,' it hardly matters how many opportunities a policy affords them to say so" (Chait and Ford 1982, p. 46). On balance, it is equally important to recognize and to act on those occasions when it is appropriate to say "yes."

REFERENCES

The ERIC Clearinghouse on Higher Education abstracts and indexes the current literature on higher education for the National Institute of Education's monthly bibliographic journal, *Resources in Education*. Most of these publications are available through the ERIC Document Reproduction Service (EDRS). For publications cited in this bibliography that are available from EDRS, ordering number and price are included. Readers who wish to order a publication should write to the ERIC Document Reproduction Service, 3900 Wheeler Avenue, Alexandria, Virginia 22304. When ordering, please specify the document number. Documents are available as noted in microfiche (MF) and paper copy (PC). Because prices are subject to change, it is advisable to check the latest issue of *Resources in Education* for current cost based on the number of pages in the publication.

American Association of University Professors. 1977. *AAUP Policy Documents and Reports*. Washington, D.C.: American Association of University Professors. ED 136 646. 105 pp. MF–$1.19; PC–$9.55.

———. 1978. "On Full-time Non-Tenure-Track Appointments." *AAUP Bulletin* 64(3): 267–73.

———. 1979. "Academic Freedom and Tenure: University of Texas at Permian Basin." *Academe* 65: 240–50.

American Council on Education. 1984. *1984–85 Fact Book on Higher Education*. New York: MacMillan.

Atelsek, Frank, and Gomberg, Irene. 1980. *Tenure Practices at Four-Year Colleges and Universities*. Washington, D.C.: American Council on Education. ED 190 015. 49 pp. MF–$1.19; PC–$5.64.

Bagshaw, Marque. 1984. "Faculty Staffing Practices at Four-Year Colleges and Universities." Doctoral dissertation, Pennsylvania State University.

Baldwin, Roger. 1981. "Planning and Action on Campus." In *Expanding Faculty Options: Career Development Projects at Colleges and Universities,* edited by Russell Edgerton. Washington, D.C.: American Association for Higher Education. ED 217 780. 114 pp. MF–$1.19; PC not available EDRS.

Bleau, Barbara L. 1982. "Faculty Planning Models: A Review of the Literature." *Journal of Higher Education* 53(2): 195–206.

Bloomfield, Stefan D. 1977. "Comprehensive Faculty Flow Analysis." In *Applying Analytic Methods to Planning and Management,* edited by David S. Hopkins and Roger G. Schroeder. New Directions for Institutional Research No. 13. San Francisco: Jossey-Bass.

Bloomfield, Stefan D., and Updegrove, Daniel A. 1981a. "Modeling for Insight, Not Numbers." In *Management Science Appli-*

cations to Academic Administration, edited by James A. Wilson. New Directions for Higher Education No. 35. San Francisco: Jossey-Bass.

———. 1981b. "A Modeling System for Higher Education." *Decision Sciences* 12: 310–21.

Bottomley, Wayne N. 1978. "The USC Faculty Planning Model: A History and Description." Unpublished paper. Los Angeles: University of Southern California. ED 185 882. 7 pp. MF–$1.19; PC–$3.89.

Bottomley, Wayne N.; Linnell, Robert H.; and Marsh, Herbert W. 1980. "Differences in Cost, Tenure Ratio, and Faculty Flow as a Result of Changes in Mandatory Retirement Ages." *Research in Higher Education* 13(3): 261–72.

Bowen, Frank M., and Glenny, Lyman A. 1976. *State Budgeting for Higher Education*. Los Angeles: University of California, Center for Research and Development in Higher Education. ED 122 721. 8 pp. MF–$1.19; PC–$3.89.

———. 1981. "The California Study." In *Higher Education Financing Policies: States/Institutions and Their Interactions*, edited by Larry Leslie and James Hyatt. Tucson: University of Arizona, Center for the Study of Higher Education. ED 215 614. 170 pp. MF–$1.19; PC not available EDRS.

Carnegie Council on Policy Studies in Higher Education. 1975. *More than Survival: Prospects for Higher Education in a Period of Uncertainty*. San Francisco: Jossey-Bass.

———. 1976. *A Classification of Institutions of Higher Education*. Rev. ed. Berkeley, Calif.: Author. ED 217 742. 150 pp. MF–$1.19; PC–$13.06.

———. 1980. *Three Thousand Futures: The Next Twenty Years for Higher Education*. San Francisco: Jossey-Bass. ED 183 076. 175 pp. MF–$1.19; PC not available EDRS.

Centra, John A. 1977. "Faculty Development Practices." In *Renewing and Evaluating Teaching*, edited by John A. Centra. New Directions for Higher Education No. 17. San Francisco: Jossey-Bass.

———. 1979. *Determining Faculty Effectiveness: Assessing Teaching, Research, and Service for Personnel Decisions and Improvement*. San Francisco: Jossey-Bass.

Chait, Richard P. 1976. "Nine Alternatives to Tenure Quotas." *AGB Reports* 18(2): 38–43.

———. 1979. "Tenure and the Academic Future." In *Tenure: Three Views*. New Rochelle, N.Y.: Change Magazine Press. ED 177 951. 57 pp. MF–$1.19; PC–$7.39.

———. 1984. "Academic Personnel Policy and Administration." In *Trustee Responsibility for Academic Affairs*, edited by

Richard P. Chait and associates. Washington, D.C.: Association of Governing Boards of Universities and Colleges.

Chait, Richard P., and Ford, Andrew T. 1982. *Beyond Traditional
Tenure: A Guide to Sound Policies and Practices.* San Francisco: Jossey-Bass.

College and University Personnel Association. 1980. "Tenure and
Retrenchment Practices in Higher Education: A Technical
Report." *Journal of the College and University Personnel
Association* 31: 1–226.

Commission on Academic Tenure in Higher Education (the Keast
Commission). 1973. *Faculty Tenure: A Report and Recommendations.* San Francisco: Jossey-Bass.

Davis, Carolyne K., and Dougherty, Edward A. 1978. "Program
Discontinuance: Its Role in Strategies of Resource Allocation
and Planning for Colleges and Universities." Mimeographed.
Ann Arbor: University of Michigan. ED 153 553. 17 pp. MF–
$1.19; PC–$3.89.

Di Biase, Elaine R. 1979. "Classical Tenure and Contemporary
Alternatives: Academe's Principles and Court Decisions."
Doctoral dissertation, Pennsylvania State University.

Dickmeyer, Nathan. 1983. *Financial Conditions of Colleges and
Universities.* Washington, D.C.: American Council on Education and National Association of College and University Business Officers. ED 227 753. 73 pp. MF–$1.19; PC not available
EDRS.

Dougherty, Edward A. 1979. "What Is the Most Effective Way to
Handle Program Discontinuances?: Case Studies from 10 Cam-
puses." Paper presented at the AAHE annual conference,
April, Washington, D.C. ED 181 789. 42 pp. MF–$1.19; PC–
$5.64.

———. 1980a. "University of California–Riverside." Unpublished manuscript. Ann Arbor: University of Michigan.

———. 1980b. "University of Wisconsin." Unpublished manuscript. Ann Arbor: University of Michigan.

Eddy, Edward D., and Morrill, Richard L. 1975. "Living with
Tenure without Quotas." *Liberal Education* 61: 399–417.

Edgerton, Russell. 1981. "The Need to Rethink Faculty
Careers." In *Expanding Faculty Options: Career Development
Projects at Colleges and Universities,* edited by Russell Edger-
ton. Washington, D.C.: American Association for Higher Edu-
cation. ED 217 780. 114 pp. MF–$1.19; PC not available
EDRS.

El-Khawas, Elaine, and Furniss, W. Todd. 1974. *Faculty Tenure
and Contract Systems: 1972 and 1974.* Washington, D.C.:
American Council on Education. ED 100 197. 35 pp. MF–
$1.19; PC–$5.64.

Ernst, Richard J., and McFarlane, Larry A. 1978. "Are We Shortchanging Our Students by Using Part-time Faculty?" In *Employing Part-time Faculty,* edited by David W. Leslie. New Directions for Institutional Research No. 18. San Francisco: Jossey-Bass.

Evangelauf, Jean. 12 December 1984. "Enrollments Stable This Fall." *Chronicle of Higher Education* 29: 1+.

Fortunato, Raymond T., and Waddell, D. Geneva. 1981. *Personnel Administration in Higher Education.* San Francisco: Jossey-Bass.

Fulkerson, William. 1974. *Planning for Financial Exigency in State Colleges and Universities.* Washington, D.C.: American Association of State Colleges and Universities. ED 112 803. 68 pp. MF–$1.19; PC–$7.39.

Furniss, W. Todd. 1974. "Steady-State Staffing and Issues for 1974." *Educational Record* 55: 87–95.

Gappa, Judith M. October 1984a. "Employing Part-time Faculty: Thoughtful Approaches to Continuing Problems." *AAHE Bulletin* 37: 3–7.

———. 1984b. *Part-time Faculty: Higher Education at a Crossroads.* ASHE-ERIC Higher Education Research Report No. 3. Washington, D.C.: Association for the Study of Higher Education. ED 251 058. 129 pp. MF–$1.19; PC–$13.06.

Gillis, John W. October 1971. "Academic Staff Reduction in Response to Financial Exigency." *Liberal Education* 57: 364–77.

Gray, John A. 1981. "Legal Restraints on Faculty Cutbacks." In *Challenges of Retrenchment: Strategies for Consolidating Programs, Cutting Costs, and Reallocating Resources,* edited by James Mingle and associates. San Francisco: Jossey-Bass.

Gray, Paul. May 1977. "University Planning Models: A Survey and Bibliography." Council of Planning Libraries, Exchange Bibliography 1279.

———. 1980. "A Faculty Model for Policy Planning." *Interfaces* 10(1): 91–103.

Hammond, John S. 1974. "Do's and Don'ts of Computer Models for Planning." *Harvard Business Review* 52(2): 110–23.

Heim, Peggy. 1980. "The Economic Decline of the Professoriate in the 80's: What Happened to Faculty Salaries and What Are the Implications?" *Current Issues in Higher Education* 3: 12–20. ED 194 006. 26 pp. MF–$1.19; PC not available EDRS.

Heller, Scott. 21 November 1984. "Growing Pains at Texas Tech: Faculty and President Clash over Tenure." *Chronicle of Higher Education* 29: 19–22.

Hendrickson, Robert M., and Lee, Barbara A. 1983. *Academic Employment and Retrenchment: Judicial Review and Administrative Action.* ASHE-ERIC Higher Education Research Report No. 8. Washington, D.C.: Association for the Study of Higher Education. ED 240 972. 133 pp. MF–$1.19; PC–$13.06.

Hopkins, Daniel S. P. 1972. *An Early Retirement Program for the Stanford Faculty: Report and Recommendations.* Palo Alto, Calif.: Stanford University. ED 083 947. 72 pp. MF–$1.19; PC–$7.39.

———. 1974. "Faculty Early-Retirement Programs." *Operations Research* 22: 455–67.

Hopkins, Daniel S. P., and Massy, William F. 1981. *Planning Models for Colleges and Universities.* Stanford, Calif.: Stanford University Press.

Ingalls, Zoe. 9 January 1985. "Early Retirement Option in New York State Attracts Hundreds of College Employees." *Chronicle of Higher Education* 29: 27.

Jacobson, Robert L. 9 January 1985. "Cost of Fringe Benefits in 1983 Averaged 18.6 Pct. of Payrolls." *Chronicle of Higher Education* 29: 27+.

Jenny, Hans H.; Heim, Peggy; and Hughes, Geoffrey C. 1979. *Another Challenge: Age 70 Retirement in Higher Education.* New York: TIAA/CREF. ED 177 940. 86 pp. MF–$1.19; PC–$9.56.

Jenny, J. R. 1974. *Early Retirement, A New Issue in Higher Education: The Financial Consequences of Early Retirement.* New York: TIAA. ED 095 759. 53 pp. MF–$1.19; PC–$7.39.

Johnson, Mark D., and Mortimer, Kenneth P. 1977. *Faculty Bargaining and the Politics of Retrenchment in the Pennsylvania State Colleges, 1971–1976.* University Park, Pa.: Pennsylvania State University, Center for the Study of Higher Education. ED 148 201. 112 pp. MF–$1.19; PC–$9.15.

Johnstone, James N. 1974. "Mathematical Models Developed for Use in Educational Planning: A Review." *Review of Educational Research* 44(2): 177–201.

Katz, Daniel A. 1977. "Tenure Ratios under Conditions of Positive or Negative Faculty Growth." *AAUP Bulletin* 63: 301–3.

Keller, George. 1983. *Academic Strategy: The Management Revolution in American Higher Education.* Baltimore: Johns Hopkins University Press.

Knodle, L. L.; Noval, Lois; Powell, James; Rogers, Frederick; and Updegrove, Daniel. 1979. "EFPM: Users' Experiences at Purdue University, Oberlin College, and Carnegie-Mellon University." *EDUCOM Bulletin* 14(2): 5–11.

Kreinen, Mordechai E. 1982. "Preserving Tenure Commitments in Hard Times: The Michigan State Experience." *Academe* 68(2): 37–45.

Ladd, Everett C., Jr., and Lipset, Seymour M. 17 November 1977. "Many Professors Would Postpone Retirement if Laws Were Changed." *Chronicle of Higher Education:* 16.

Leslie, David W.; Kellams, Samuel E.; and Gunne, Manny G. 1982. *Part-time Faculty in American Higher Education.* New York: Praeger.

Leslie, Larry L. 1984. "Bringing the Issues Together." In *Responding to New Realities in Funding,* edited by Larry L. Leslie. New Directions for Institutional Research No. 43. San Francisco: Jossey-Bass.

Linnell, Robert H., and Bottomley, Wayne N. 1975. "The USC Faculty Model." Unpublished paper. Los Angeles: University of Southern California. ED 179 142. 61 pp. MF–$1.19; PC–$7.39.

Linnell, Robert H., and Gray, Paul. 1977. "Faculty Planning and Affirmative Action." *Journal of the College and University Personnel Association* 28(2): 6–9.

Lozier, Gregory G. 1977. "Negotiating Retrenchment Provisions." In *Handbook of Faculty Bargaining,* edited by George W. Angell, Edward P. Kelley, Jr., and associates. San Francisco: Jossey-Bass.

MacDonald, Puring O. 1980. "An Appraisal of Early Retirement Programs and Prospects at Penn State." Mimeographed. University Park, Pa.: Pennsylvania State University, Office of Planning and Budget.

Magarrell, Jack. 1 June 1983. "Growth in State Funds for Colleges Expected to Slow in 1984." *Chronicle of Higher Education* 26: 1+.

———. 9 May 1984. "Growth of States' Tax Revenues Expected to Slow Next Year." *Chronicle of Higher Education* 28: 14.

Masland, Andrew T. 1983. "Simulators, Myth, and Ritual in Higher Education." *Research in Higher Education* 18(2): 161–77.

———. 1984. "Integrators and Decision Support System Success in Higher Education." *Research in Higher Education* 20(2): 211–33.

Melchiori, Gerlinda S. 1982. *Planning for Program Discontinuance: From Default to Design.* AAHE-ERIC Higher Education Research Report No. 5. Washington, D.C.: American Association for Higher Education. ED 224 451. 58 pp. MF–$1.19; PC–$7.39.

Meléndez, Winifred A., and de Guzmán, Rafael M. 1983. *Burn-out: The New Academic Disease*. ASHE-ERIC Higher Education Research Report No. 9. Washington, D.C.: Association for the Study of Higher Education. ED 242 255. 114 pp. MF–$1.19; PC–$11.31.

Mingle, James R. 1982. "Redirecting Higher Education in Times of Budget Reduction." *Issues in Higher Education* 18: 1–5.

———. 1983. "Management Flexibility and State Regulation: An Overview." In *Management Flexibility and State Regulation in Higher Education*, edited by James R. Mingle. Atlanta: Southern Regional Education Board. ED 234 705. 65 pp. MF–$1.19; PC–$7.39.

Mitchell, Barbara A. 1981. "Faculty Early Retirement: A Planning and Budgeting Issue in Higher Education." In *Higher Education Planning and Budgeting: Ideas for the 80's*, edited by Melodie Christal. Boulder, Colo.: National Center for Higher Education Management Systems. ED 213 351. 147 pp. MF–$1.19; PC–$13.06.

Morisseau, James J. 1973. "Simulation Models in Higher Education." *Planning for Higher Education* 2(3): 5.

Mortimer, Kenneth P. 1981. "Procedures and Criteria for Faculty Retrenchment." In *Challenges of Retrenchment: Strategies for Consolidating Programs, Cutting Costs, and Reallocating Resources*, edited by James R. Mingle and associates. San Francisco: Jossey-Bass.

———. 1984. "Academic Programs." In *Trustee Responsibility for Academic Affairs*, edited by Richard P. Chait and associates. Washington, D.C.: Association of Governing Boards of Universities and Colleges.

Mortimer, Kenneth P.; Bagshaw, Marque; and Caruso, Annette. 1985. *Academic Reallocation: A National Profile*. University Park, Pa.: Pennsylvania State University, Center for the Study of Higher Education.

Mortimer, Kenneth P.; Caruso, Annette C.; and Ritchey, Thomas I. 1982. "The Faculty and the Institution: A Question of Context, Terminology, and Linkages." Mimeographed. University Park, Pa.: Pennsylvania State University, Center for the Study of Higher Education..

Mortimer, Kenneth P., and Ladd, Everett C. 1981. "Faculty." In *Higher Education: A Bibliographic Handbook*, vol. 2, edited by D. Kent Halstead. Washington, D.C.: National Institute of Education. ED 238 307. 672 pp. MF–$1.76; PC–$45.30.

Mortimer, Kenneth P., and McConnell, T. R. 1978. *Sharing Authority Effectively*. San Francisco: Jossey-Bass.

Mortimer, Kenneth P., and Taylor, Barbara E. 1984. "Budgeting Strategies under Conditions of Decline." In *Responding to New Realities in Funding*, edited by Larry L. Leslie. New Directions for Institutional Research No. 43. San Francisco: Jossey-Bass.

Mortimer, Kenneth P., and Tierney, Michael L. 1979. *The Three R's of the Eighties: Reduction, Reallocation, and Retrenchment*. AAHE-ERIC Higher Education Research Report No. 4. Washington, D.C.: American Association for Higher Education. ED 172 642. 93 pp. MF–$1.19; PC–$9.56.

National Commission on Student Financial Assistance, Graduate Education Subcommittee. 1983. *Signs of Trouble and Erosion: A Report on Graduate Education in America* ("Brademas Report"). New York: New York University. ED 239 546. 87 pp. MF–$1.19; PC–$9.56.

Nevison, Christopher H. 1980. "Effects of Tenure and Retirement Policies on the College Faculty: A Case Study Using Computer Simulation." *Journal of Higher Education* 51(2): 150–66.

Nollen, Stanley D.; Eddy, Brenda B.; and Martin, Virginia H. 1977. *Permanent Part-time Employment: The Manager's Perspective*. Washington, D.C.: Georgetown University, School of Business Administration.

Olswang, Steven G. 1983. "Planning the Unthinkable: Issues in Institutional Reorganization and Faculty Reductions." *Journal of College and University Law* 9(4): 431–49.

Patton, Carl V. 1976. "Early Retirement in Academia: Making the Decision." *The Gerontologist* 17(4): 347–54.

———. 1979. *Academia in Transition: Mid-Career or Early Retirement*. Cambridge, Mass.: Abt Books.

———. 1983. "Institutional Practices and Faculty Who Leave." In *College Faculty: Versatile Human Resources in a Period of Constraint*, edited by Roger G. Baldwin and Robert T. Blackburn. New Directions for Institutional Research No. 40. San Francisco: Jossey-Bass.

Perry, Susan. 21 September 1983. "Formal Reviews for Tenured Professors: Useful Spur or Orwellian Mistake?" *Chronicle of Higher Education* 27: 25–26.

Peterson, Marvin W. May/June 1984. "In a Decade of Decline: The Seven R's of Planning." *Change* 16: 42–46.

Plourde, Paul J. 1976. "Institutional Use of Models: Hopes or Continued Frustration?" In *Assessing Computer-Based Systems Models*, edited by Thomas R. Mason. New Directions for Higher Education No. 9. San Francisco: Jossey-Bass.

Roark, Anne C. 20 March 1978. "Universities Could Lose Millions in Research Pay." *Chronicle of Higher Education* 16: 4.

Schroeder, Roger G. 1974. "Resource Planning in University Management by Goal Programming." *Operations Research* 22: 700–10.

Shapiro, Harold T. September 1978. "Resource Planning and Flexibility." *Business Officer:* 20–23.

Spinney, David L., and McLaughlin, Gerald W. 1979. "The Use of a Markov Model in Assessment of Alternative Faculty Personnel Policies." *Research in Higher Education* 11(3): 249–62.

Sprenger, Joanne M., and Schultz, Raymond E. 1974. "Staff Reduction Policies." *College Management* 9: 22–23.

Stadtman, Verne A. 1980. *Academic Adaptations: Higher Education Prepares for the 1980s and 1990s.* San Francisco: Jossey-Bass.

Stokey, Edith, and Zeckhauser, Richard. 1978. *A Primer for Policy Analysis.* New York: W.W. Norton & Co.

Strohm, Paul. 1981. "Faculty Responsibilities and Rights during Retrenchment." In *Challenges of Retrenchment: Strategies for Consolidating Programs, Cutting Costs, and Reallocating Resources,* edited by James R. Mingle and associates. San Francisco: Jossey-Bass.

Study Group on the Conditions of Excellence in American Higher Education. 1984. *Involvement in Learning: Realizing the Potential of American Higher Education.* Washington, D.C.: National Institute of Education. ED 246 833. 127 pp. MF–$1.19; PC–$13.06.

Toombs, William E. 1983. "Faculty Development: The Institutional Side." In *College Faculty: Versatile Human Resources in a Period of Constraint,* edited by Roger G. Baldwin and Robert T. Blackburn. New Directions for Institutional Research No. 40. San Francisco: Jossey-Bass.

Tuckman, Barbara H., and Tuckman, Howard P. March 1980. "Part-timers, Sex Discrimination, and Career Choice at Two-Year Institutions." *Academe* 66: 71–76.

Tuckman, Howard P. December 1978. "Who Is Part-Time in Academe?" *AAUP Bulletin* 65: 305–15.

Tuckman, Howard P., and Caldwell, Jaime. November/December 1979. "The Reward Structure for Part-timers in Academe." *Journal of Higher Education* 50: 745–60.

Vaupel, James W. 1981. "Over-Tenured Universities: The Mathematics of Reduction." *Management Science* 27(8): 904–13.

Waggaman, John S. 1983. *Faculty Recruitment, Retention, and Fair Employment: Obligations and Opportunities.* ASHE-ERIC Higher Education Research Report No. 2. Washington, D.C.: Association for the Study of Higher Education. ED 227 806. 73 pp. MF–$1.19; PC–$7.39.

ASHE-ERIC HIGHER EDUCATION REPORTS

Starting in 1983, the Association for the Study of Higher Education assumed cosponsorship of the Higher Education Reports with the ERIC Clearinghouse on Higher Education. For the previous 11 years, ERIC and the American Association for Higher Education prepared and published the reports.

Each report is the definitive analysis of a tough higher education problem, based on a thorough research of pertinent literature and institutional experiences. Report topics, identified by a national survey, are written by noted practitioners and scholars with prepublication manuscript reviews by experts.

Eight monographs (10 monographs before 1985) in the ASHE-ERIC Higher Education Report series are published each year, available individually or by subscription. Subscription to eight issues is $55 regular; $40 for members of AERA, AAHE, and AIR; $35 for members of ASHE. (Add $7.50 outside the United States.)

Prices for single copies, including 4th class postage and handling, are $7.50 regular and $6.00 for members of AERA, AAHE, AIR, and ASHE ($6.50 regular and $5.00 for members for reports published before 1983). If faster 1st class postage is desired for U.S. and Canadian orders, add $.75 for each publication ordered; overseas, add $4.50. For VISA and MasterCard payments, include card number, expiration date, and signature. Orders under $25 must be prepaid. Bulk discounts are available on orders of 15 or more reports (not applicable to subscriptions). Order from the Publications Department, Association for the Study of Higher Education, One Dupont Circle, Suite 630, Washington, D.C. 20036, (202) 296-2597. Write for a complete list of Higher Education Reports and other ASHE and ERIC publications.

1982 Higher Education Reports

1. Rating College Teaching: Criterion Studies of Student Evaluation-of-Instruction Instruments
   Sidney E. Benton

2. Faculty Evaluation: The Use of Explicit Criteria for Promotion, Retention, and Tenure
   Neal Whitman and Elaine Weiss

3. The Enrollment Crisis: Factors, Actors, and Impacts
   J. Victor Baldridge, Frank R. Kemerer, and Kenneth C. Green

4. Improving Instruction: Issues and Alternatives for Higher Education
   Charles C. Cole, Jr.

5. Planning for Program Discontinuance: From Default to Design
   Gerlinda S. Melchiori

6. State Planning, Budgeting, and Accountability: Approaches for Higher Education
   Carol E. Floyd

7. The Process of Change in Higher Education Institutions
   Robert C. Nordvall

8. Information Systems and Technological Decisions: A Guide for Non-Technical Administrators
   Robert L. Bailey

9. Government Support for Minority Participation in Higher Education
   Kenneth C. Green

10. The Department Chair: Professional Development and Role Conflict
    David B. Booth

1983 Higher Education Reports

1. The Path to Excellence: Quality Assurance in Higher Education
   Laurence R. Marcus, Anita O. Leone, and Edward D. Goldberg

2. Faculty Recruitment, Retention, and Fair Employment: Obligations and Opportunities
   John S. Waggaman

3. Meeting the Challenges: Developing Faculty Careers
   Michael C. T. Brookes and Katherine L. German

4. Raising Academic Standards: A Guide to Learning Improvement
   Ruth Talbott Keimig

5. Serving Learners at a Distance: A Guide to Program Practices
   Charles E. Feasley

6. Competence, Admissions, and Articulation: Returning to the Basics in Higher Education
   Jean L. Preer

7. Public Service in Higher Education: Practices and Priorities
   Patricia H. Crosson

8. Academic Employment and Retrenchment: Judicial Review and Administrative Action
   Robert M. Hendrickson and Barbara A. Lee

9. Burnout: The New Academic Disease
   Winifred Albizu Meléndez and Rafael M. de Guzmán

10. Academic Workplace: New Demands, Heightened Tensions
    Ann E. Austin and Zelda F. Gamson

1984 Higher Education Reports

1. Adult Learning: State Policies and Institutional Practices
   K. Patricia Cross and Anne-Marie McCartan

2. Student Stress: Effects and Solutions
   Neal A. Whitman, David C. Spendlove, and Claire H. Clark

3. Part-time Faculty: Higher Education at a Crossroads
   Judith M. Gappa

4. Sex Discrimination Law in Higher Education: The Lessons of the Past Decade
   J. Ralph Lindgren, Patti T. Ota, Perry A. Zirkel, and Nan Van Gieson

5. Faculty Freedoms and Institutional Accountability: Interactions and Conflicts
   Steven G. Olswang and Barbara A. Lee

6. The High-Technology Connection: Academic/Industrial Cooperation for Economic Growth
   Lynn G. Johnson

7. Employee Educational Programs: Implications for Industry and Higher Education
   Suzanne W. Morse

8. Academic Libraries: The Changing Knowledge Centers of Colleges and Universities
   Barbara B. Moran

9. Futures Research and the Strategic Planning Process: Implications for Higher Education
   James L. Morrison, William L. Renfro, and Wayne I. Boucher

10. Faculty Workload: Research, Theory, and Interpretation
    Harold E. Yuker

1985 Higher Education Reports

1. Flexibility in Academic Staffing: Effective Policies and Practices
   Kenneth P. Mortimer, Marque Bagshaw, and Andrew T. Masland

INDEX

A

Abramson v. Board of Regents, University of Hawaii, 38
Academic deans, attitude toward reallocation, 3
Academic Flow Model, 63
Academic freedom, 23
Academic staffing
    contingency perspective, 80
    faculty consulting, 85
    flexibility, 15–58
    flow models, 59–70
    informed choices, 81
    institutional strategy, 80–81
    institutional values, 81–82
    managerial prerogatives, 86
    nonmonetary rewards, 85–86
    realistic expectations, 82
    relationship to fiscal affairs, 83
    tenure track management, 83–85
Accountability to government, 7
Accreditation jeopardy, 83
Admissions policies, 11
Affirmative action
    goals, 50
    model use for planning, 66–67
Age Discrimination in Employment Act, 8, 47
American Association of University Professors, 23–25, 36–38, 41,
    48, 49, 51, 52
American Federation of Teachers, 41
Annuity enhancements, 43
Association of American Colleges, 48
Attrition
    as reallocation/reduction strategy, 71–72
    to control academic positions, 19–21

B

Benefit payments, as incentive for retirement, 43
Budget reduction, 12. *See also* Reallocation and reduction
Buyouts, 44

C

California state university system, 40
Career assessment, faculty, 53
Career change. *See* Faculty retraining/reallocation
Carnegie classification, 3, 9
Carnegie-Mellon University, 66
Censure of institutions, 23–25

NOTES

NOTES

NOTES

NOTES